PRAISE FOR
DIGITAL DARWINISM

'A fascinating dip into a disruptive future.' **Dylan Jones, Editor, *GQ***

'This finally answered many questions about innovation which have long
haunted me – not least why most large companies are typically so bad at it.
It's one of those rare books that is worth reading twice.' **Rory Sutherland,
Vice Chairman, Ogilvy & Mather Group, and TED speaker**

'In a cacophony of voices calling for an immediate digital revolution, how reassuring
to hear one advocating a more nuanced and balanced path forward for your business.
How refreshing to have an author parting the weeds of digital transformation,
offering homespun, achievable suggestions and solutions for your company.

The digital world is littered with a baffling array of jargon and acronyms.
Goodwin cuts through the gobbledygook to offer down-to-earth, practical advice
for transforming your business. *Digital Darwinism* reassures you that futurizing
your company doesn't mean you need to be the next Uber or Amazon of
anything. Among the multiple platinum nuggets in this book, the most valuable
takeaway is that change must be at the core of your business, not at the edges.
Digitally transform your business? First change the way you think about change.'
Adam Najberg, Head of Digital Media, Alibaba; formerly Digital Editor,
The Wall Street Journal Asia

'In *Digital Darwinism*, Goodwin presents a thoughtful canvas of digital wisdom,
covering the past, present and future with smart illustrative examples. It's a great
map of the entire digital landscape, sprinkled with invaluable insights to act
upon.' **Stefan Olander, former Vice President, Global Digital Innovation, Nike**

'The future does not fit in the containers or mindsets of the past. This book
persuades, provokes and points to ways to rethink your business. Society,
business and life are being disrupted by a revolutionary stage of evolution:
Digital Darwinism. This book provides ways to thrive in the new environment.'
**Rishad Tobaccowala, transformation expert, speaker and writer, and
Chief Growth Officer and member of the Management Committee,
Publicis Groupe**

'Goodwin delivers what he promises in his preface: the book is wildly irritating and inspiring at the same time. It is a passionate cry for more common sense in corporate decision making. The examples he provides demonstrate how little companies have embraced the digital age. Goodwin rightly questions the attempts from corporations to overcome disruption and ambiguity in the digital age either by "better planning" or by minor adjustments to business models and strategies that were developed in a bygone era of stability, linearity and predictability. He reminds us that a flexible response is the only answer to massively changing corporate environments and that entrepreneurship means maximizing opportunities and overcoming obstacles instead of minimizing risks. An overdue book.' **Uwe Ellinghaus, former Global Chief Marketing Officer, Cadillac**

'*Digital Darwinism* is a must-read for both legacy brands and ambitious start-ups, arming business leaders with clear strategies to navigate disruption, unlock growth and prepare for the future. A bold and provocative thinker, Tom Goodwin brings a fresh approach and a much-needed reminder that you have to think differently in order to win in today's global digital economy.' **Stefan Larsson, former CEO, Ralph Lauren**

'Tom Goodwin sees organizations facing a Darwinian battle for survival, given the pace of technical change. That's familiar ground. What's so refreshing is his notion that empathy will be crucial in that battle – that businesses that put people first are most likely to stay the right side of the chaos.' **Mark Jones, Commissioning Editor, the *World Economic Forum Agenda*; formerly Global Editor, Networked Journalism, and Global Communities Editor, Reuters News**

'Tom Goodwin shows how Darwinian success depends not on ruthlessness but on learning how to play well with others.' **Douglas Rushkoff, author, *Throwing Rocks at the Google Bus***

'Goodwin is the right kind of futurist: he's a history geek at heart, and recognizes that innovation doesn't happen in a vacuum. Context is king, and there's plenty of that in this intelligently constructed book.' **Paul Kemp-Robertson, Co-founder, *Contagious***

'If you ever wondered if and how you and your organization could survive and grow in today's disruptive environment this is the book for you. This beautifully written book offers an informative and insightful description of the age of disruption, the need for a paradigm shift in our thinking and practical guidelines for survival and growth. Enjoy, learn and apply.' **Jerry Wind, The Lauder Professor Emeritus of Marketing, The Wharton School, University of Pennsylvania**

'Today the words "disruption" and "innovation" are plastered everywhere. We've become numb to them, lost in a sea of information. The future is here yet it is understood unequally. With *Digital Darwinism*, Tom Goodwin uses his unique combination of passion, empathy and audacity to give us all an equal understanding of the future as it bowls over us.' **John Winsor, thinker, advisor and entrepreneur building platforms in the marketing, media and innovation industries, and Founder and CEO, Open Assembly**

DIGITAL DARWINISM

Survival of the fittest in the age of business disruption

TOM GOODWIN

Kogan Page
INSPIRE

Publisher's note

Every possible effort has been made to ensure that the information contained in this book is accurate at the time of going to press, and the publisher and author cannot accept responsibility for any errors or omissions, however caused. No responsibility for loss or damage occasioned to any person acting, or refraining from action, as a result of the material in this publication can be accepted by the editor, the publisher or the author.

First published in Great Britain and the United States in 2018 by Kogan Page Limited

2nd Floor, 45 Gee Street	c/o Martin P Hill Consulting	4737/23 Ansari Road
London EC1V 3RS	122 W 27th St, 10th Floor	Daryaganj
United Kingdom	New York NY 10001	New Delhi 110002
	USA	India

www.koganpage.com

© Tom Goodwin, 2018

The right of Tom Goodwin to be identified as the author of this work has been asserted by him in accordance with the Copyright, Designs and Patents Act 1988.

ISBN   978 0 7494 8228 2
E-ISBN   978 0 7494 8229 9

British Library Cataloguing-in-Publication Data

A CIP record for this book is available from the British Library.

Library of Congress Cataloging-in-Publication Data

CIP data is available.

Library of Congress Control Number: 2018003915

Typeset by Integra Software Services Pvt. Ltd., Pondicherry
Print production managed by Jellyfish
Printed and bound by CPI Group (UK) Ltd, Croydon, CR0 4YY

CONTENTS

And in closing 201

PREFACE

Welcome to my first book.

This is a sentence I never expected to write; I am an unlikely writer of anything. It was never my dream to be a thought leader of any sort, or to speak at events. The words flow from my fingers – not as part of some romantic mission, lofty goal or stubbornly unticked item on a bucket list – but because I care. This book is reluctant; it's driven by a huge need to get some ideas out there, to prompt a debate, to explore a new way to connect ideas and a new way to see change in the world.

Despite having published 250 articles in the last two years, writing this book has been the hardest thing I've ever done. I've rarely demanded more than 30 minutes of someone's attention so the pressure I feel to keep you interested for the hours it takes to read this book is huge. I'd guess that the best authors are empathetic enough to be riddled with self-doubt. Do I have enough to say? Is this new and profound? Is this both interesting and valuable? Do I have the right balance of naivety and confidence, knowledge and freshness to question things from an un-entrenched view? As my passions run deep I'm constantly wondering if I care too much or not enough, if I'm being objectively critical or just plain miserable. This book is not here to be cathartic, but enlightening.

Above all else I wondered if this book should consist of entirely new thoughts or if I should just take some of the most provocative, interesting and well-received pieces from before and weave a strand of new thinking to join them up. In the end this book is a mixture. I started with a blank sheet of what I wanted to say, a holistic narrative to best aid companies in uncertain times, but embellished with some extracts of some of my best-performing work. This book is a new journey, occasionally touching upon some familiar territory on the way. I hope this feels reassuring, rather than repetitive.

To be sure that you can follow this journey, I've done my best to structure it very clearly. There are three themes to this book, covering the past, present and the future. Each has three chapters covering different lessons, ideas, theories or viewpoints. In addition to these nine chapters there is a chapter to introduce the ideas I've explored and to provide a platform for understanding, as well as a final chapter to focus what has been discussed and to send you on your way.

A fast-changing world

I'm sure that those living through the Agrarian Revolution must have waxed lyrical about 'these fast-moving times' and those visiting the first thrusting skyscrapers in early 1900s New York would without doubt have felt an incredible sense of excitement and acceleration of life. But it is this current moment that feels like the greatest time ever to be alive. We are in an age where existential changes are sweeping through many aspects of the world around us. Where incredible things we once could barely dream about are quickly becoming possible. Where the lifespan, health and wealth of the population of the world improves far more quickly than we ever expected. Where the cost of batteries and solar power and other foundational elements that will propel mankind into a new era are plummeting faster than even the most optimistic projections ever thought. These are times where optimism should be rife and where excitement should be palpable. We should in every industry wake up fresh and energized and inspired by this – but it rarely feels that way.

We see the rise of fake news, striking workers threatened by Uber or robots or zero-hours contracts. We see companies declaring bankruptcy at an alarming rate or mergers of the hopeful with the hopeless. Countless columns spread the fear of what artificial intelligence (AI) will bring to us, people talk about taxation on robots and the idea of the universal basic income. We explore challenges that seem different to those before them, more pervasive, more substantial, more existential. AI is threatening to take the jobs of 'people like us'. From the rise of wealth inequality to increasing political intolerance or religious extremism, we can feel the world creaking under change.

It feels like a planet on a threshold. The proximity of abundance and health abruptly rubs against despair. While the developed world seems to look confidently into the future, much of the West seems uncomfortably drawn to nostalgia and the comfort of the past. The tensions between optimism and sheer panic are everywhere. The internet should be killing ignorance, spreading tolerance and empathy, and yet feels weaponized to foster extremist views that feel normalized. Is globalization a good thing; is migration helping diversity; is freedom growing; is the power of Google, Apple, Facebook, Amazon (GAFA) becoming too great, too fast, and are they beyond the reach of government now?

Taking on the consensus

These vast questions combined with the unlimited education available on the internet should lead to great debate. Yet I don't see it happening.

I see casual consensus on most fronts. My passion for writing this book comes from a great sense of frustration. I feel passionately that so much of what we speak of in the broader business environment is utter nonsense and that so much of the writing of today is merely groupthink. I feel passionately that better questions lead to better work and more significant progress. I get frustrated with the vacuousness of conversations and the lack of discourse for good. In times when things seem chaotic, most people are so keen to feel that they understand the world, that they blindly accept what appears to make sense without challenging it. I'd prefer a little more Socratic debate and a little less thoughtless and automatic retweeting.

When I read about the worlds of business and marketing, advertising or technology, I'm bowled over by the lack of real conversations about the big issues, and by the platitudes and the quasi-academic thinking that is rife in so many business books. In this book I'm going to be inquisitive and subversive. I'm going to question the works of people far brighter, far more experienced and far more knowledgeable than I am. Hopefully I'm going to challenge *you*. I'm going to get you to ask deep, existential and even naive questions. The questions people don't ask because they know they are so hard, it seems both stupid and rude to ask them. I've always believed that the best innovation consultants don't stick endless post-it notes on a wall or do three-part mapping exercises or sit on funky sofas with a white board: they are like eight-year-old kids who never stop asking why, don't know any better and are unforgiving of excuses because they are idealists.

The journey starts here

It took four years of thinking and research to write this book in six months. It's been written on trains in Norway, in conference centres in Peru, hotels in Sydney, bars in rural Turkey. Elements come from the top floor of skyscrapers in Dubai, others from weird street cafés in Delhi or small villages in Umbria. I've been inspired in Auckland, confused in Colombia, and enlightened in rural Romania.

I'm lucky to have a role that allows me to speak, write, observe and listen around the world, and I learn the most from listening. My job is to connect dots, to see commonalities and differences. This book is based on what I've learned from reading the local newspapers in Canada, listening to worried workers in Shenzhen, speaking to government officials in Spain or chatting over dinner in Curitiba. Ideas and themes in this book have come together from this breadth and depth.

Having done this, I find it impossible not to see the common themes, the panic, excitement and energy all over the world. What increasingly bonds people, in ways they perhaps don't know, is the contrast between hope and fear, the sense of confusion about change. This book is designed to make the complexity of this moment feel simple. It is meant to separate the changes that matter from those that don't. It's designed to draw from the past in order to understand the future, to look at what is changing and, most of all, what is not. It's here to be angry with what we're currently doing, because what we can soon accomplish will be amazing. More than anything else, this book is for those keen to have their hand held through the chaos of this moment of peak complexity.

This book has been a balancing act. I've tried to weave a path between personal opinions and more substantiated and academic thinking. I've aimed to cover enough material to keep it interesting, but in enough depth to make it useful. I hope to ask questions, seed ideas and cover potential solutions, yet this book is not here to provide all the answers. It's not my place to do that. I've written it the only way I know how. I've made it challenging, personal and hopefully light-hearted. It is deliberately irritating, because this is a time when we need to challenge conventional thinking, to explore tensions we prefer not to, and I'm happy to aggravate to get vital conversations started.

So, sit back. I hope you are as wildly irritated as you are inspired. I hope you are entertained and informed. I hope you agree wildly and disagree massively at different points on this journey, and more than anything else, I hope I inspire you to think differently and share your opinions on these stimuli, with me and anyone else you see fit.

For the majority of industries, those with key roles in business face two choices. Manage the decline or rebuild and prosper. I know which one I'd rather do and this book is here to help.

THANK YOU

I want to thank my family and friends, so long as they forgive me for being a terrible person to be around for the last year. Having a book inside you is like being pregnant in your head. I've carried this in my brain for so long that it's made me selfish, grumpy and inside myself.

I want to say thank you for the replies I got from my provocation on social media that led to so many conversations that I learned from.

I want to thank my Mum and Dad, for basically always believing in me, but putting no pressure on me. For making me the pain in the neck with good intentions that I am, for instilling in me the belief that everyone and everything should be challenged, but in a nice way, and that listening is more important than talking. I want to thank Shann Biglione, Nick Childs and Adi Kurian for their advice at key times in the making of this book.

And I want to especially and specifically thank Adriana Stan, who believed in me from day one and when I didn't. For spotting a degree of talent in me and for nurturing it. You inspired and supported me to write several years ago and you are behind (in some shape or form) pretty much all of the success I have had today in writing and speaking.

Business in the age of disruption

'I wouldn't start from here'

There is a tale about a man who, lost in the deepest country lanes of rural Ireland, approaches a passer-by herding sheep along the single-track lane. Winding down the window, the man asks for directions to Dublin. The local takes a long deep breath and thinks long and hard before replying, 'Well sir, if I were you, I wouldn't start from here'.

It's not the best joke, but it's a reasonable metaphor for business today. When faced with the winds of change, many of us are unstable, saddled with a legacy of what were well-intentioned and reasonable decisions but which now, in retrospect, feel unwise. This resulting cumulative effect means many businesses are simply not fit to compete with other younger companies today. With no clear sign of a path ahead, I wonder how many businesses wish they could start from somewhere else?

Companies, like people, are manifestations of all the decisions ever made. They are the result of years of accumulating employees, acquiring businesses, inheriting assets, systems, cultures. For many years the pace of change was sufficiently slow that these lumbering beasts could adapt over time. Leaders would construct new units, managers would start new initiatives, change could be bolted on. Yet three things have happened.

The world has changed

As a species, human beings are designed to live in a world that is local and linear; yet the pace of change has increased, change is now global and exponential, yet companies are largely the same. The world appears to change more drastically and more quickly than ever, and in many ways that pace of change is accelerating. At the same time, the ability of many companies to change and adapt has not speeded up. So many companies are not agile enough to reconfigure, re-engineer or otherwise change as quickly as consumer expectations and the business environment demand, or as fast as their competitors can.

Secondly, the advantages of size have slowly crumbled. Big companies have forever leveraged huge advantages over smaller companies. They could negotiate vast discounts on costs of goods, they could leverage their position to gain distribution, they could spend vast sums on advertising, attract the best staff, borrow money whenever needed. The internet and changing business dynamics now mean that slowly many of the benefits of being large are being wiped out. In fact, increasingly, what once made companies powerful, like ownership of assets, expertise, large workforces, historical brands, are to some extent becoming liabilities and make change harder.

Thirdly, we've seen thrusting insurgent companies built for the modern age change the market. We've observed the rise of companies that have ignored all known wisdom. They have built themselves with the latest technology at their core, they have skirted round or ignored prior regulations and bent the rules. They are constructed on new economic principles and counter-intuitive business models that have treated legal and societal responsibility as externalities. These companies often have lower operating costs, scale fast, and have often removed value from entire markets. Experience has always been seen as a good thing, yet now it is those companies built most recently, with the latest technology embedded deeply at the very core of their business, that seem to offer the best structure for growth in the future.

It's these three changes – rapid global change, the irrelevance of size, and the rise of insurgent companies – above all else that now make life different. They mean that companies have to think hard, be bold and challenge themselves. In this chapter I want to introduce the main concepts of Digital Darwinism, how it can drive and contextualize business transformation, and better address change in the modern world. I want to get businesses to start asking the right questions: the hard, existential ones. This chapter is about understanding the context and reason for change, while providing a wider foundation for concepts that I build on in later chapters.

It's time to ask the hard questions

The most profound and the very best questions we never dare to ask are: what would your business look like if it was created today? What would it do? How would it do it? How would it make money? What would you still have done and what would you never have created? These are questions about your company's very existence, best posed in a holiday home in a foreign land, or staring out of the train window, well removed from the realities of day-to-day working.

If your answer is that your business would be exactly the same if set up today, then either you are not thinking hard enough, or you've set up your company this weekend, or most worryingly, you are ignorant of many of the changes in the world and what is now possible.

The answers will most likely be annoying. You probably feel irritated now. You may feel a little judged and misunderstood and don't like the tone I am using. Your department or business has probably worked extremely hard to weather change, to adapt incrementally, and to create a sensible balance between modernization and capital expenditure. More than likely it's not perfectly placed for today's world, but not so badly placed that people are enduring frequent sleepless nights. It's likely positioned considerably worse for the future, but the day-to-day struggles mean you rarely get a chance to look that far ahead.

Your company probably never really had a 10-year plan. Its mission statement is probably one that kept everyone happy, not one that was surgically focused and empowering. Your company is unlikely to have done future planning to see change coming and build for it. Your company is likely to be the best that could be done, given modern realities.

Most companies are like the tax code or Heathrow Airport. They are the aggregation of countless alterations, additions, patches and workarounds that have accumulated over years. Each incremental change is based on sound thinking and the realities of each moment and each one allows the business to just about work. Yet the UK tax code is 17,000 pages long; Heathrow is a mess and in the wrong place. Both would be far better if they could be started again.

The next question to ask is: can you carry on like this? At what point in size or inefficiency does it make sense to go back to the drawing board? Your business may be able to function each day, but for how long will that be the case? We know deep down that, one day, Heathrow won't exist, that car makers will need to make electric cars, that many retailers will need more efficient mechanisms to supply direct online. We know that TV companies will have to change at some point, that banks can't carry on as they are. Advertising and marketing will one day have to rethink its structure, as will energy or tobacco companies, but for how long can they resist? There are of course some sectors that may not face great change: mining, timber, farming, water provision will of course face change, but probably not to the same level of chaos, threat and opportunity.

These questions are best followed by more progressive and helpful questions. What can you do to get to that place? Can you get there with what you have, or do you need to start again? Who and what will help make this happen? How can this realistically be done?

The Silicon Valley idiom of 'building the plane while you're flying it' is rather nonsensical, but somehow companies do need to think of their succession strategy. Do they build a new system and switch over to it one day, or can they re-engineer what they have? Perhaps they should just create a new entity in a new category. As these chapters progress, my intention is to fan the flames of intrigue, be irritating to the point of bringing desire to change, but then follow up with reasonable steps of how to get there.

We have to get better at looking forward. We can learn from the past and the failure of Kodak or Nokia, Blockbusters or Borders, but these stories have been told many times over and the dynamics of today are different. For years physical retailers didn't worry about Amazon because it was different, it was for 'online shopping' – how silly this looks now. If Facebook has access to 2 billion people on this planet, it can quickly become a retailer or entertainment company; if people trust Google, there is nothing to stop it becoming a bank. A key part of preparing to change is looking forward, not backwards.

Remember what is not changing

The hardest part of my role is maintaining balance. While things may be changing faster, the reality is that not everything is different; in fact far, far more aspects of our lives are the same. You are still looking at a dead tree with ink right now (unless you have the e-book edition!).

Change is indeed here, but not uniformly distributed. The lives of middle-class people in Mumbai, Sydney, Manila, Tokyo, New York and London seem to become ever more similar to each other, while becoming ever more different to the lives of those in the rural areas surrounding them. Increasingly, rural dwellers around the world are facing challenges which are more similar to each other than those facing rural and city dwellers in the same country.

Because of the nature of the world, most people who will be reading this book are going to be rather more like me and like each other than what we might term 'typical'. Equally, we would probably be regarded as 'atypical' in comparison with 'average' folk. Even in 2018, even in developed nations, the 'average person' does not buy groceries online, they do not rent apartments on Airbnb. An average person does not send others money via their phones or own a 'smart speaker'. We need to remember that one-third of people in the USA still rent and buy video on DVDs (Rodriguez, 2017), and as late as mid-2015 only one in seven of US adults had used Uber, Lyft or another ride-sharing platform (Smith, 2016). We 'non-average' readers live massively unrepresentative lives and we need to remember this and change our viewpoint.

Trend lines are important. It's likely that DVDs will die out, ride-sharing will become more popular and spread out to rural areas. It's likely we will use our voices more to interact with computers. We will continue to buy more stuff not from physical stores but online, electric propulsion will change the face of car-making and the businesses that serve it. Yet the underpinning of human civilization will not change. Brands and our need to form social bonds by expressing who we are, or to aid selection by trust, are not going to vanish because of Amazon. Airlines are not going to go bankrupt because they don't have staff wearing augmented reality (AR) headsets, hotels won't suddenly implode because they don't have connected speakers in the room.

When I sit drinking a Pilsner in a Frankfurt beer hall, it's obvious that family-run breweries that hark back to 1695 are not facing looming existential crises. I don't think they need innovation sessions to establish what 3D printing or virtual reality (VR) headsets could mean for their company, just as I don't think they suffer sleepless nights about what the 'Uber of beer' could be for them.

My role is to decide what is changing and what matters, knowing what to change and also what not to. I firmly believe it is not necessarily the case that technology has changed everything or will do so in the future. If you are a milk brand, a baker or hairdresser, it's not obviously the case that radical change is on the horizon, or that when it does appear it will be rapid and catastrophic. Companies that own coffee brands and make ground coffee for retailers don't necessarily need to become 'tech companies that happen to make coffee'. Not every company will look manifestly different.

We tend not to hear nuanced views on the future because in words widely attributed to Bob Hoffman, 'Nobody ever got famous predicting that things would stay pretty much the same' (The Ad Contrarian, 2017). Yet even those who presume change won't affect them, even those who are furthest away from the technologies we read about most often, would still be wise to keep their eyes open ahead, even if it's so they can be manifestly more comfortable changing nothing, or so they can embrace the power of what's next, despite not having to.

Change is a threat at a core level

When we ask what your business would look like if it was started today we have to be brutal and honest. We have to penetrate to the core of what companies are about, we have to question the foundations of companies and then look at that in the context of the changing world. We have to examine the reason companies exist and the core tenets and principles on which they are built.

Modern businesses can be visualized as skyscrapers. They exist on vast foundations, built in the shape and with the techniques that the best thinking at the time suggested would be most effective and sensible and that supports what the building is projected to be.

The location of the skyscraper's foundation is set by optimizing for local and global knowledge, economic forces and a sprinkling of what's been learned through years of best practice.

On this foundation, a huge steel or concrete frame is built that projects up into the air, forming the main structural elements and outlining the shape and function of the building.

The steel or concrete framework of this building is a metaphor for the organizational form of companies. These are the organizational elements of business, the departmental structures, the rules, the core elements that make businesses the way they are, that create their physicality, what they make, how they make it, the operational and business models.

Built on top of this and fixed into place around the main structural elements are the service elements, the lifts, the fire escapes, the service corridors and the plumbing, electrical wiring, heating and air systems. In this metaphor, they represent the culture and processes of business today. They are the way that the building or business operates, the pulse of the building or company, the lifeblood that makes it work.

Finally, on this vast foundation, fixed in place by the structural elements, serviced and contextualized by the service elements, are the more visible, more decorative elements. These include the interior design, the furniture, the reception area's look and feel, the indoor plants, the choice of paint colour, and so on. In this metaphorical skyscraper, it is the funky chairs in the lobby, the artwork in the toilets, the corporate film that plays in reception and the small details that augment the visitor's experience of the company.

In a business, represented by this building, these elements are the equivalents of what the company does to represent itself. They are where the building meets the guests, or where the company markets itself. The marketing, the branding, the press releases, the advertising, everything which is the outermost representation of what a company does. This is what people see most readily: it's the most superficial aspect of design, but also what most efficiently represents what the company wants to be. Now, for both the building and the business it represents, it's this visual garnish, this superficial layer, that is both the easiest thing to change as well as the most illusory – in effect an efficient way of changing appearance rather than what really matters.

In a world that changes faster and more significantly than ever, when we consider this analogy we have to ask: what does a business do when it's not in the right place? What if the skyscraper made sense in London, but now should be in São Paulo? What if it was built to house 1,000 highly-paid workers who would only ever dream of working in Manhattan in a prestigious tower, and now outsourcing means most jobs should be in Bangalore?

What happens if the foundation was planned to support a 30-storey building, but as needs grew we just added new storeys haphazardly on top? What happens if the framework was constructed for brick walls and we now want large windows? What happens if regulations mean that we need another fire escape? What if the elevators are not made to serve so many workers? What if we don't need any workers any more?

In fact, the world of construction offers many metaphors for businesses. The UK has spent billions of pounds maintaining old train lines, rather than building new high-speed lines. Today's expensive, slow and at-capacity train lines are the result of years of incremental change. They result from what was a steady flow of investment, not a large single investment that would have been harder to get approved. They exist because the work could be done continuously and not take 10 years to build and it would reduce the extent of the disruption. They exist because nobody had the courage to make a difficult decision that would have taken a long time to show the results.

The reality is that the shifting nature of business has created an environment of change where modern business models, new technologies, new consumer behaviours and new competitors mean that the large lumbering infrastructure of businesses increasingly looks like the wrong thing, built in the wrong place, based on old thinking. In this metaphor, in many cases most of what companies have constructed is now entirely unhelpful. Today, new companies that have started from scratch and are built on new thinking, systems, code, technology and culture are making old businesses look archaic.

We see legacy issues all over the world, manifesting themselves in very different ways and at very different scales. We have retailers that wish they didn't own stores, entertainment companies that wish they'd bought global rights when they made content, car companies that wish they'd not invested in billion-dollar combustion engine plants or owned dealership networks. I often see successful but empty restaurants and wonder if the owners wish they could just use Seamless or Grubhub and not rent a vast space where people once sat. The role of these businesses seems to have shifted. We have banks that don't want to be tied down to the regulation of what being a bank means, airlines that wish they didn't have unionized workers, and many companies that wish they didn't have any workers.

Sometimes these cracks are small: taxi companies who call themselves 'AAA Cars' to get placed at the front of the Yellow Pages; expensively procured memorable phone numbers; and hoarding medallions worth over a million dollars that were once a very safe investment. Change affects business owners but can also affect individuals. Again, using just taxis as a single example, black cab drivers in London have to learn 'the knowledge' and buy very expensive official vehicles. Ride-sharing apps have not altered these needs; they have obliterated them. Google Maps didn't make spending between two and four years learning the knowledge merely a bit less helpful; it destroyed its value overnight by not only undermining the value in knowing street names, but also by supplying real-time traffic information, making the decades of experience and knowledge of the fastest routes redundant. A taxi business is not changed by technology, it's turned on its head. The best starting point for a taxi company today is a blank sheet of paper, and not an old taxi company that can be changed.

The degree of change required, the company's wrong location, the expense, time and risk involved in making these changes means that paralysis strikes and we favour fast, easy illusions of change: decoration, not foundation – wallpapering over the cracks.

As this pace of change in life accelerates, legacy businesses are going to find it harder, not easier to keep up. At some point, rather like Heathrow Airport, or JFK in New York, one wonders if it would not be better to start again, not make changes to what you have.

If you were to replace Heathrow, you'd build a replacement airport before closing it. You'd build in a far better location, not requiring the most delicate flightpath manoeuvres over central London. You'd construct it with far more capacity for growth. You would build it with modern consumer needs in mind: it would be constructed with the very latest software and using the most advanced construction techniques known. It would be designed to be opened to take over the old airport, to be its future. It would open before the old one closed, it would both increase the future potential of the airport, but also stop the damage and wastage that would have happened if it had not been constructed.

This is self-disruption. It's expensive, it appears unnecessary, it's risky, takes time and it's not what is generally done. We prefer to modify, to hope, to reduce the chance of things going wrong. Self-disruption is to own your future, before it's too late, and by building the future of your company. It means hard decisions, making deep existential changes and perhaps even undertaking activity that appears to be cannibalistic in nature.

Self-disruption

Your biggest risk isn't occasional failure; it's sustained mediocrity.
WROBLEWSKI, 2017

One of the strangest flips in the modern world is that the internet has rewired the playing field. The assets that once made companies successful in the Industrial Age now often appear to work against you in the Digital Age. Often the metrics that once mattered most – profitability, revenue – seem to have become less vital than the potential for the future. The market's valuation of Uber or Amazon is based more on trajectory than reality, on user growth, not the proven ability to make money from them. These are baffling times. For a long time legacy companies have been comforted by assets that are increasingly becoming liabilities.

In my TechCrunch piece titled 'The Battle is for the Customer Interface', I stated:

Uber, the world's largest taxi company, owns no vehicles. Facebook, the world's most popular media owner, creates no content. Alibaba, the most valuable retailer, has no inventory. And Airbnb, the world's largest accommodation provider, owns no real estate. Something interesting is happening.

Goodwin, 2015

It was this quote that many felt summarized the changing dynamics in the world. It is clear that companies need to change. To accomplish significant and sustained profitable growth in the 21st century, companies will have to explore more than mere incremental improvements to existing business models. They will have to do more than line filling or small innovations with a few new products. Compared with explosive new entrants that set the market expectations, these actions just won't generate enough growth anymore.

Expectations are changing. The share prices of large retailers, especially department stores, show that confidence in legacy businesses is waning. The ascent of Tesla's stock price relative to large, experienced US car companies shows the same. It is also true for customer expectations: we no longer tolerate lost bookings, or waiting in line to pay.

Neither the market nor the customers are forgiving. You can have both excuses and explanations for your inability to function like nimble businesses built today, but the stock market and customers won't care for long. They need action.

We're in the age of innovation as distraction

Any innovation that is undertaken is usually the most outward-facing, physical and quick. In our metaphorical skyscraper, it's like installing new artwork or refurnishing the staff canteen when the building is about to fall. We live in a time of innovation as gesture. From an Apple Watch app to fancy ad campaigns using artificial intelligence to chatbots, innovation is less about making a meaningful difference to consumer experiences, and more about broadcasting to the marketplace, the trade press and the stock market that they get it. Innovation today is done with the goal of virtue signalling rather than commercial payback. Robots used in trial stores do allow for learning and data capture, but most likely they're there to make a nice image in the annual company report. A VR headset used to showcase a hotel room of the future makes a great video to stick on YouTube, flying a Boeing 747 with some biofuel in one engine still gets picked up on TV. Change gets merchandised and companies merely create a veneer of newness. It's not deep or behind the scenes; it's always tangible manifestations of what we think the body language of innovation should look like. For large companies, innovation in 2018 is just building an innovation lab, doing regular 'Silicon Valley safaris', 'working with start-ups' and always releasing a press release of intent, never one of accomplishment.

We need proper change and the time is now. This shift is vital and the gap between what is known to be required and what is done is huge. A 2016 KPMG study highlighted how 65 per cent of CEOs are concerned about new entrants disrupting their business models and 53 per cent believed they aren't disrupting their own business models enough (KPMG, 2016). In one McKinsey study, 80 per cent of CEOs believed their business models to be at risk; and only 6 per cent of executives were happy with their company's innovation performance (McKinsey, 2013).

The depth of change is underestimated

Companies that need to change are everywhere and the depth of change is often misunderstood. If you were to start a media company such as a newspaper today, it's not just that you wouldn't own paper mills or that you wouldn't employ hundreds of expensive senior writers, staff photographers or fact-checkers, like the *New York Times* once did. Having non-unionized workers, a cheaper headquarters, making more clickable pieces and employing younger and cheaper staff would also probably not be enough. Employing the best data scientists, making software that sees what stories are sparking and creating more of those, making native content with brands, would all still not be enough to make money. These would all aid your survival and increase the likelihood of the death being slow, but this isn't how you'd want to think about it.

No, if you were to start a media company today, you'd want to replicate Facebook or Snapchat or Twitter. You'd make nothing and be a thin horizontal layer between people who want stuff and people who make stuff. You'd record vast amounts of data, sell advertising automatically to the highest bidder, you'd take no responsibility for any content that appeared on the site and reduce all externalities, whether costs or responsibility. You'd be able to scale globally at the touch of a button and you'd scale to add video.

A legacy media business can't get to this place by retooling. It needs to start from nothing. Memory, expertise, skills and relationships are not just unhelpful, they are likely to be problematic.

Media owners are not alone in their need to change everything. Will physical retailers with huge global footprints and distribution systems ever be able to bolt on new distribution systems that can serve customers direct to their homes? More than this, will they be able to do so in a way that meets modern consumer expectations for price and speed while still making their unit costs profitable? Or would they be better off starting from nothing?

Do car makers need to swallow the fact that their incredibly vast knowledge of combustion engines and complex organizational system of suppliers and sub-suppliers may not only be unhelpful but may even sabotage their developments in a world of electric cars? Will they be able to succeed in a world where electric cars are assembled more like smartphones, not fabricated like cars of the past? Will large car companies ever grasp that cars are becoming more like electronics, with value in the software rather than the hardware, and where user interfaces are now a primary consideration for the buyer? Will car companies understand that vehicles may soon be 'accessed' like data on a mobile tariff, rather than owned? That the holistic ownership experience – how you buy the car, get it serviced, renew the lease – may be more important than just the car itself?

Guts are required to understand that disruption isn't about superficial changes; it's about rebuilding the entity that will revolutionize what your current company does. It's not about managed decline or reducing costs to meet profit goals. It's about a leap of faith, investment in the future of what your business needs to be. It's a process best described as 'self-disruption' – undertaking the bold changes needed, at a core level, to best prepare yourself for a new future. The goal of self-disruption is to become the entity that eats your own company's future, rather than having someone else do it.

The evolution of business is somewhat like the evolution of species. It's a series of small incremental changes to develop optimal results.

It's about mutations from the norm that make change possible. It's testing and learning, trial and error, a sudden shift to a different approach where new forms and functions suddenly appear. In this world, the organizations that are the most adaptable, the most freeform and the fastest at changing will be the ones most likely to survive. It is a time where being responsive to the environment, to shifting consumer needs and to wild new industry entrants is crucial. Being able to learn, knowing when to stick and when to shift and, above all else, having a vision is what will propel a company forward. In the words of Jeff Bezos about Amazon, 'We're stubborn on vision and flexible on details' (Levy, 2011).

The only issue with evolution as a basis for change is that we now live in a time when the forces of nature are greater and the time spans are shortened. Businesses tend to operate not so much as species that evolve gradually across the planet, but in an environment which undergoes great shifts.

The only certainty now is uncertainty

Changes to the world are not just happening faster, but in more haphazard and unexpected ways. On the day this chapter was written, one Bitcoin was worth $11,000, when I checked the final version four months later, the price had sunk to $8,500, after reaching $19,700 six weeks prior to that. Quite honestly nobody has the remotest idea what will happen to its value in future. Those who explain it do so based on little more than faith. By the time you read this the price could be 100 times less, or more, or zero; we have no idea how this currency and the technology beneath it will develop, and even less understanding of what it will mean and how it will change.

It appears that few saw Brexit coming, or the results of the 2017 US presidential election. The rise in the Dow Jones Index in late 2017 seems odd. Fidget spinners come and go and the Ice Bucket challenge dies. Pokemon Go went from the 'next big thing' to 'remember that?' in about two months. 3D-printing companies' share prices slump, and the Amazon Echo appears from nowhere to become the hit of 2017. Unlikely things seem to be likely. For years we've assumed it's the pace of change that is the biggest problem for business; these days it increasingly feels like it's unpredictability. Today few people in few industries can make personal or business decisions based on the assumption that the world will remain within 'norms'. The standard deviation of life seems to be increasing, and technologies come together in so many new ways that it's hard to see how new patterns will emerge.

Will something like Magic Leap, a headset base that augments reality experience, launch and make TVs seem anachronistic? Will self-driving cars happen sooner than expected and spread faster than predicted and change the fundamentals of urban development? Will 3D printing undermine the entire retail landscape? Will drones make infrastructure on the ground seem short-sighted? The cost of solar panels has already plummeted far faster than even the most optimistic projections, so this seems like a bad time to have committed to build a nuclear power station. Global climate could be worse or different than anyone expects and quite honestly, we've no idea what this will mean for the future.

Today the world does seem like it's on some sort of threshold. We've had smartphones for around 10 years and we can't imagine life without them, but we've also no idea what their impact will be. We don't know how they change childhood and brain development or what they mean for education. They could unlock incredible human capital and wealth around the world. Or, on the contrary, they could espouse our fears and create more barriers. We seem to have a declining middle class in much of the world, richer rich people – it's a soup that's both explosive and unpredictable. When human lifespans reach over 100 years, what new problems will emerge? What about the housing market and intergenerational wealth transfer? Will Millennials finally have some cash to spend with the advertisers that have been trying to reach them for years?

We need to remember, however, that life is destined to become more complex and chaotic: the laws of physics and entropy suggest that there is no alternative. As technology breeds ever more choices, the range of options gets wider, and the number of ways in which new things can coalesce and combine becomes greater. A skill for all companies in the future will be to exist in such uncertainty, to be prepared for reasonable eventualities but not to be paralysed by indecision and fear. In life it's best to focus only on what actually matters and what we can control. One way to do this is to think less about the ever-changing world and more about what Bill Bernbach would call the unchanging man.

It's time to focus on people

Innovation is not disruptive; consumer adoption is.
JEFF BEZOS (BISHOP, 2017)

Management consultants traditionally have done a great job of helping businesses through periods of change. They have been excellent at understanding new technology and management theory and, while facing the CEO and other senior staff, have helped companies produce things more efficiently, cheaper and perhaps at a higher quality. These consultancies have done an excellent job of understanding the business and creating incremental change.

These are different times. Change requires companies to step change rather than incrementally improve. The world's best candle-makers continually made better candles, but they never invented the lightbulb. Today companies need to leap to new business models and rethink fundamentals and what they stand for, not slowly tweak what has worked before. Management consultants still practise thinking developed in the 1960s and 70s for the Industrial Age. They've changed little in that time; even the Boston Matrix is 47 years old.

Part of the issue is that management consultancies serve the needs of the business, not of the consumer. It's their job to provide reassurance, to have all the answers and for them to be indefatigable. Yet being certain often means you are not applying the right amount of imagination, not exploring far enough. The world needs consultancies to work around the needs of the consumer, consultancies that foster new thinking, that look ahead not to the past, that look around the world not to the textbooks.

More than in any other era I see now a greater need for empathy and imagination and not traditional consulting. Businesses constructed for the wrong era on the wrong foundations will not thrive because of a tweaked customer relationship management (CRM) system or a new data strategy, despite that being the easiest project to sell in.

The benefits of the Internet of Things – or 5G, or real-time tracking, or cloud computing, or any one of the big topics large consultancies love to present leadership on – will only work for companies bold enough to re-imagine what they do and for those that are working around modern customer needs, who create services that people want, and who create customer experiences that are best-in-class.

More than anything else I would love this book to be a wake-up call to those in innovation agencies or digital consultancies and especially in advertising agencies to regain the seat in the boardroom, to stand bold and believe in yourself. This is your time to make a difference.

Key topics to inspire

This book comprises three themes: one focusing on the past and what we can learn, another on what can be done and is happening today, and the third and final theme looking ahead into the future. Each of these themes holds three chapters that represent different contexts or elements to consider. There are five key notions that are vital to the book's message. It is these five topics, covered in the following section, that should be the clear takeaways from this work.

Digital Darwinism

The overarching principle of this book is Digital Darwinism, the umbrella concept that wraps up all the strands of thought and the background for every idea and principle discussed. The idea of Digital Darwinism is that, like any species, companies are designed to improve slowly over time, to optimize, to breed selectively, to become better via rather slow but consistent and well-proven evolution.

This has worked for large and small businesses alike, but things are different now. The pace of technological and societal change has now become so fast that the background for business changes faster than any company can. Natural adaptation and typical agility are no longer enough. Companies now need to look further ahead, to try to be not just agile, but predictive, to be comfortable being uncomfortable, and to be constantly finding ways to change the core essence of what they are. They need to embrace risk. Business today needs a new style of leadership, a new way of thinking about remuneration, a new way to change culture. It requires new approaches to technology, to using data, to understanding people. While not all businesses are facing threats to their existence, many of them are or soon will be, and the waves of change are spreading outwards faster than ever before. In this position you can either manage the decline as best you can, or boldly rethink and re-imagine yourself for the future. If you want to do the latter, then here are some principles to consider.

Mid-digital age

Up to now, we've been in the early stages of digital transformation. We don't think of it that way: we've had smartphones for 10 years, we're used to ride-share apps, mobile banking, social media. It feels like we've lived with this stuff for a while. Generally speaking, however, we've added digital garnish to what we've known before. Most TV shows are 30 minutes long because they had ad breaks, yet streaming no longer requires this. Stores talk about 'checking out' and 'baskets', we have 'desktops' and 'trash' on our laptops. We've generally taken the thinking, the units and processes from the past and, with the smallest amount of effort, digitized them. We're in a period where a lot of it doesn't work, for anyone. We often drop calls, we can't get on Wi-Fi as the landing page is slow, many industries have lost billions in profit and the world has not yet come to terms with globalization or the casualization of the workforce. We are in the stage of peak complexity.

We're in a hybrid period between two ages. We live in an analogue world augmented by the new possibilities of digital, but not rethought or rebuilt for this era. It's this existence in two systems – where we can both watch TV and stream the same show, pay with Apple Pay but have to swipe our pen to sign to authorize payment, learn online but see the value of a degree diminish – that shows how messy life is. It seems likely that one day things will make sense, that the world will work, that we won't have e-passports or mobile boarding passes or e-tickets, we will just pay or access with our faces. We won't use cash because it won't exist, we won't use set-top boxes for TV because with 5G our phones will become our gateway to all content. One day, things *will* work and we need to start thinking about how we'd construct things for that world now.

Digital at the core

In 2006 the world's largest companies were primarily energy companies, banks and large industrial conglomerates like General Electric. In fact, on Bloomberg's list of the top 10 largest companies in the world in 2006, most were over 50 years old, employed large workforces, and only one was labelled a 'tech' company. By 2016 things were radically different: only two companies remained on the list and five of the largest were categorized as technology companies (*The Economist*, 2016).

From Amazon to Apple, Alphabet (Google's parent company) to Microsoft, Facebook to China Mobile, most of these companies are relatively young but have also grown massively in the last few years. While we like to think of these as 'tech' companies I think it's a strange term. Facebook and Google make more than 95 per cent of their revenue and profit from selling advertising, so they are media owners. Apple makes consumer electronics. What these companies have in common is that they were built from the ground up with digital thinking at the core. By 'digital thinking' I mean both an understanding of technology but also evolved consumer behaviour. Companies that have been constructed for the business environment of today, with technology at their core, have been the most successful and this becomes a valuable way to think about how to become the company you need to be.

Paradigm leap

Every design project needs a brief, but it also needs assumptions; to question everything would take too long. So, like every creative endeavour, design processes follow both convergent and divergent phases. We go wide and then we hone down to an optimum solution. During this process we use these assumptions to shape what we do. This explains why, when we look around us, most things are similar. Most four-door saloon cars look broadly similar, most bank lobbies feel the same, as do the products they offer. Airbus jets are not radically different to Boeing or Bombardier airplanes, much as American Airlines' business class is much the same as Delta's. Websites tend to have the same layout, retailers create stores on the same rules... you get the idea.

There are times when companies, often companies that are new to a sector, break all the rules. Tesla makes cars that change all the automotive rules: the Model S has fewer than 20 moving components in total, whereas a typical combustion engine car has nearly 1,500 moving parts and takes one-sixth the time to assemble (Sawhney, 2017; O'Connor, 2013). They sell cars direct not via dealers. The problems they need to solve are entirely different to those found in the previous paradigm; they need software engineers not transmission experts, they need to build charging grids not repair infrastructure. The most successful companies today are not those steeped in experience, but those with no experience, who asked stupid questions. Facebook said, why do we need to make content? Apple asked, shouldn't a phone be a delight to use? Amazon said, but why do we need to sell only our own inventory? Trump asked, what if a politician didn't act like a politician? The most successful companies today are the ones with the courage to challenge rules, who build themselves on different assumptions, who challenge the status quo, but do so based on the next paradigm, not the last. It is companies who hope to survive by making small incremental changes that now lose out to the ones that bet big on radical innovation and change.

Leapfrogging

The concepts of building with digital at the core and unleashing the power of the paradigm leap go alongside the next idea in this book, the concept of the leapfrog.

Technology tends to operate within paradigms. We lived in the age of water power, then steam, then electricity and now we're in the digital age. We used shells as money, then coins, then paper notes and now we use digital currency. The UK saw the age of cargo by horse, then by canal, then by railway and now by road. Computing shifts from local personal computers, to local mainframes, to cloud-based systems and databases, yet we're perhaps on the edge of new decentralized systems using blockchain technology.

As we travel the world we see the power of building a country or company on the very latest technology and the most recent business environment and consumer landscape. The most advanced trains in the world are in China, as is the fastest-growing renewable energy programmes; digital currencies took root in Kenya before they did in the USA; the first passenger drones are likely to be in Dubai; Estonia by some measure has the most advanced government infrastructure and governance thanks to building an entire system in the last few years based on blockchain technology.

Today's successful companies have often become so by investing significant resources in a particular system that, when it becomes outdated, proves very costly to repair or change. If the USA were discovered today it probably would not have spent $500 billion on the US interstate highway system (Planes, 2013). According to a US Department of Transportation report, just maintaining current highways and bridges until 2030 will cost a cool $65.3 billion – per year – and that's being conservative; instead it might have spent the same amount on self-driving cars that can use narrower roads (Abruzzese, 1988; Marshall, 2017). If China had waited a few more years, it could have built a rail network with Hyperloop technology and spent perhaps 10 times less than the $500 billion it's currently spending to connect the nation with high-speed trains (Medlock, 2017; Davies, 2013). It also seems that increasingly the answer to problems in the future won't be expensive hardware, but better software. Perhaps in 2026, after the UK spends $23 billion on a new runway at Heathrow, we will discover that better software could have increased the capacity on two runways for a far lower cost, or that we no longer need to travel so much because we can explore places in virtual reality.

There comes a point where old infrastructure and systems get in the way, and the unit economics of sustaining the system don't allow for profitability. It's extremely hard even for companies built from scratch to make money from retailing online; it's even harder for those who have to modify old mechanisms, supplant ancient systems, and adapt to compete with these new entrants. Yet it's precisely when legacy companies, built for the past, face the lowest profit margins, plummeting sales and scarce investment that the greatest investment in the new is required. The frog boils to death in slowly heated water because at the very moment it needs to leap, it is most lethargic. We all need to act before it becomes vital.

Companies that are large, well-capitalized, most stable and least vulnerable need to be thinking about ways to create growth in the future and defend against young, insurgent start-ups trying to grow fast enough to irritate them. This strategy will probably not involve making huge structural shifts in a vast organization, but will require proactively working to create the entity that becomes the future of that company itself.

It's time for action

I'm not a big fan of watching cycling on the TV, but something about the Tour de France gets me excited. I love the notion of the peloton and the breakaway riders; it feels like a sensible analogy to business. For most of the time as they sweep across the sunny French landscape there is an organized group at the front, the peloton. In this lead group, riders take it in turns to be at the front; it means they pedal harder to break through the wind, while those behind can save energy due to lower air resistance. When exhausted, the leader will peel off to one side, drop to the back of the peloton and another rider will take up the lead. This feels like how businesses should operate. They should have units constantly pushing ahead, breaking into new ground, testing and learning, trying things that have not been done before, challenging conventions, and allowing the entire company to move forward. We need to embrace these pioneering riders.

So now is the time to accept unfairness, accept it's do or die, and make a plan. Can you wait it out or do you need to change? If you need to change, what is the best way? From this chapter you can see how essential it is to be poised, to be ready for change, not just to be agile, but to be predictive, and to look ahead. And to best understand the future, look at the past.

By doing that, we can avoid the mistakes of how we've applied technology incorrectly in the past and find a different way to embrace new technological developments.

References

Abruzzese, L (1988) available from: https://www.joc.com/trucking-logistics/highway-study-shows-need-increase-funding_19881006.html

Bishop, T (2017) Amazon and Blue Origin founder Jeff Bezos: 'The only thing that's disruptive is customer adoption', *GeekWire*, 7 April, available from: https://www.geekwire.com/2017/amazon-blue-origin-founder-jeff-bezos-thing-thats-disruptive-customer-adoption/ [last accessed 7 December 2017]

Davies, A (2013) available from http://www.businessinsider.com/elon-musk-hyperloop-is-10x-cheaper-than-hsr-2013-5

Goodwin, T (2015) The battle is for the customer interface, TechCrunch, 3 March, available from: https://techcrunch.com/2015/03/03/in-the-age-of-disintermediation-the-battle-is-all-for-the-customer-interface/ [last accessed 7 December 2017]

KPMG (2016) Now or never: 2016 Global CEO Outlook [online] available from: https://images.forbes.com/forbesinsights/StudyPDFs/KPMG-Global_CEO_Outlook-REPORT.pdf [last accessed 7 December 2017]

Levy, S (2011) Jeff Bezos owns the web in more ways than you think, *Wired*, 13 November, available from: https://www.wired.com/2011/11/ff_bezos/ [last accessed 7 December 2017]

Marshall, A (2017) available from: https://www.wired.com/2017/01/not-screw-spending-1-trillion-us-infrastructure/

McKinsey (2013) The eight essentials of innovation performance [online] December, available from: https://www.mckinsey.com/~/media/McKinsey/dotcom/client_service/Strategy/PDFs/The_Eight_Essentials_of_Innovation_Performance.ashx [last accessed 7 December 2017]

Medlock, K (2017) available from: https://inhabitat.com/china-is-spending-over-500-billion-to-expand-high-speed-rail/

O'Connor, E (2013) available from: http://www.businessinsider.com/how-tesla-builds-the-model-s-2013-7

Planes, A (2013) available from: https://www.fool.com/investing/general/2013/06/29/the-best-500-billion-the-united-states-has-ever-sp.aspx

Rodriguez, A (2017) Even with streaming video, a third of Americans still buy and rent, *Quartz*, 24 November, available from: https://qz.com/1136150/even-with-streaming-video-a-third-of-americans-still-buy-and-rent/ [last accessed 7 December 2017]

Sawhney, M (2017) available from: http://fortune.com/2017/05/13/tesla-market-cap-apple/

Smith, A (2016) Shared, collaborative and on demand: The new digital economy, *Pew Research Center*, 19 May, available from: http://www.pewinternet.org/2016/05/19/the-new-digital-economy/ [last accessed 7 December 2017]

The Ad Contrarian (2017) [blog] The Ad Contrarian Says, available from: http://adcontrarian.blogspot.co.uk/2017/11/no-app-for-gratitude.html [last accessed 7 December 2017]

The Economist (2016) The rise of the superstars [online], 17 September, available from: https://www.economist.com/news/special-report/21707048-small-group-giant-companiessome-old-some-neware-once-again-dominating-global [last accessed 7 December 2017]

Wroblewski, L (2017) Your biggest risk isn't occasional failure, it's sustained mediocrity [Twitter] 14 September, available from: Twitter.com [last accessed 7 December 2017]

PART ONE
Change in context

02
The electrical revolution that never was

We talk endlessly of change in the business world, but not that much is different. We still pay for things more with cash than with fingerprints. It's not that we don't have the paperless office quite yet; it's that we've never used more paper than we do today (Schwartz, 2012). Texting has been here for more than 20 years, but I can't use instant messaging to change a flight. E-mail isn't remotely new, yet I can't e-mail my bank. Mortgages are given to those with a steady work history and reams of paperwork, not those who've created a start-up that's exploding or who live a nomadic life. The world hasn't changed as much as we like to think it has. In particular, we've failed to really understand the power of digital. In this chapter I want to go back in time and, by understanding mistakes from the past, learn how best to approach today.

For over four decades electricity spread purposefully and slowly across the world, bringing small incremental changes to factories and homes, but not adding anything transformative. Most years, small incremental changes kept factory managers happy and domestic lives seemed to improve nicely. But it's only in retrospect that we can see how the transformative power of electricity was not properly harnessed.

From factory owners to workers, home owners to retailers, each and every single person thought they'd understood this new technology, and thought they'd made the necessary changes. They seemed to treat electricity as a new thing to bolt on to the side, a tweak based on small improvements, never truly digesting the meaning of this technology and working around the new possibilities it offered. It's this paradox of transformative potential vs actual change that should concern everyone in any business today.

The hard sell of electricity

It was 600 BC when the Ancient Greeks found that rubbing fur on amber (fossilized tree resin) caused an attraction between the two, and discovered static electricity. But it was only in 1831 that Michael Faraday first began generating power in a consistent, practical way. It was not long before the current was reversed and the first electric motor was born. One would expect something quite so transformative to have a near immediate effect on the world, but this was not the case. Much like the early internet, few could see the meaning at the start.

Lighting was one of the first clear and obvious applications of electricity, but it still took up to 20 years to be refined into something that was more illuminator and less fire hazard than its first iterations. By 1850, 29 years into the first steady production of electricity, the National Gallery in London as well as lighthouses around the UK coastline were lit up by electrical bulbs (The Victorian Emporium, 2011). This wasn't exactly life-changing.

Demand for electric power in households was best described as slight. Electricity was a hard sell and by the late 1800s only a very small percentage of domestic dwellings had electricity. Like most new technology it was first sold to wealthy homes as something of a gadget: first as a better way to light Christmas trees, and then a better way to light homes. In an era when the wealthy were not bothered about the workload and mental burden placed on their staff, electricity didn't seem that helpful. It was complex too. Businesses sought to take advantage of the little growth there was by trying to create their own walled gardens. A number of closed and non-compatible systems cropped up. As there was no industry-standard equipment, anyone, whether business owner, public building manager or wealthy home owner, could ask a company such as Edison or his competitors to create a custom system for their needs. Little equipment was interchangeable between makers.

The main issue remained demand. The lack of demonstrably exciting use cases meant electrical power was largely pushed onto people, not pulled by thirsty would-be customers. People buy and want solutions, not technologies. The early demise of curved TVs or Amstrad video phones shows that, unless gadgets manifest themselves as wonderful, valuable or helpful use cases, they remain frivolous and wither. The spread of electricity was slow because the use cases were underwhelming. Nobody created anything new around electrical power. The world merely took existing items and considered how they could be 'electrified'.

There was effectively no new thinking at all. We replicated the past in electrical form with no imagination; we even replicated the limitations. Gas and oil lighting had always been controlled at the light 'fixture' itself – you'd walk into a dark room, use a match to locate the light fixture and light it by hand. So the standard way to turn on electric lights was the same – use a match to find the hanging fixture and turn a switch at the base of the bulb. The idea of a wall-mounted light switch never occurred to early adopters, and then, when it was finally proposed, seemed a rather lavish and expensive feature.

A lack of both power sockets and devices to plug into them caused a curious vicious circle. How could you plug something in that had yet to be invented? And how could you create something that couldn't easily access power? The first home goods to appear were washing machines, electric vacuum cleaners, electric irons, electric refrigerators, bread toasters, and tea kettles. Slowly over time new items were invented for the electrical age and changed our relationship with electricity. Electric fans and radiant heaters created the first expectations of climate control, and electric hair dryers, telephones and radios started broadening out electricity's uses from the mere functional running of a household to really improving lifestyle.

The key way to think about power in the home was that it had many phases. First, an era of people discovering and refining a technology so that it could be used. Then a period when it was only for the rich, when its possibilities were hard to recognize, when we added power to old items to improve their functionality. Finally, a period when the technology plummeted in price, became far more accessible to all, but above all else, this was when new items were created around the potential of the technology. What started out as a way to make our Christmas trees easier for our servants to light became a technology that freed the middle classes from the hard work of running a house and put millions of women into the workforce.

Electrification of factories

Compared with the slow uptake of electricity for domestic use, and the lack of excitement that accompanied it, the electrification of factories was rapid and easily achieved. To best understand how electrical power was adopted in industry we must first understand how, where and why factories were built and how they were laid out and constructed.

The line drive system

Factories constructed from the 18th century onwards, during the Industrial Revolution, were built around a power system based on a 'line drive shaft', a huge, long, spinning shaft that would directly or indirectly power all the equipment in a factory layout. In the very first factories, this shaft was turned by water power, with waterwheels converting flowing water into an energy source. Over the course of the 18th century steam engines developed into the preferred source of power. Steam provided more torque and far more energy, was more controllable and allowed factories to be constructed anywhere people wished, so long as coal could be easily delivered in large quantities. (The first use of steam engines, rather remarkably, wasn't to directly power equipment in factories, but oddly to pump water upwards to storage reservoirs to enable waterwheels to operate. It's incredible how we tend to apply new technology to old systems.)

The line drive shaft dominated the layout of the factory. Running the entire length of any plant, it dictated virtually every aspect of the plant's design. Factories were long rectangular shapes, to ensure that all the equipment could pull power from it. Walls were massive and heavy to hold the weight of it. Huge iron reinforcement was needed, making factory construction extremely expensive. Windows for light or ventilation were very hard to make, and single-storey construction was by far the most sensible.

Figure 2.1   A cotton mill in Lancashire, 1914

SOURCE http://www.wikiwand.com/en/Cotton_mill

From the line shaft, a complex system of belts, pulleys and gears known as 'millwork', as illustrated in Figure 2.1, would ensure that all machines could be driven by the power source and would allow a small degree of control. It was possible to remove power, apply it and sometimes change the speed, all with the mere pulling of a vast lever!

Designing factories was a difficult task. Fabrication machines were not arranged in the most efficient way for the manufacture of goods, but on the most sensible layout of the machines relative to the line drive shaft. Machines requiring similar torque, speed of rotation and operating times were placed together. The vast amount of space taken up by the machines themselves, the products being made and the needs of the millwork meant that factories were incredibly tight spaces, with products frequently moving around as they made their way through the production process.

Looking at Figure 2.1, showing a typical factory in Lancashire in 2014, we can only imagine what a hazardous place this would have been in which to work: steam engines producing incredible heat and noise; huge spinning shafts making deafening noise; vibrating equipment making everything shake; no ventilation to remove heat or smells, and certainly very little natural light. Above all else, seemingly endless arrays of pulleys, belts and shafts created an extremely dangerous working environment.

The electrical shift

Factories knew how to adapt to new power sources: it had been done before. The transition from water to steam power in the Industrial Revolution in the late 1700s, first in mines, then slowly in mills, had been smooth, as existing factories with water power systems simply built on steam plants and changed the drive mechanism. New factories took the same template and built anywhere steam plants made sense.

As late as 1900 the world still considered the shift to electricity and electrical motors in the same way. By that date, less than 5 per cent of mechanical drive power in US factories was coming from electric motors. Electrical motors were a new form of power. A form of power that could offer more torque, could come on stream faster, could be cheaper and more efficient, and that required less maintenance than the many moving parts of a steam plant. It was exciting stuff.

But factory owners around the world soon did their calculations and the business case wasn't always clear. It was apparent in most cases that the energy required to run factories was a pretty small cost, often 0.5–3.0 per cent of all the running costs. The cost of the staff used to maintain steam plants wasn't exorbitant, and everyone was comfortable with what they knew. It wasn't perfect, but it was familiar. Moving to electrical motors came with the risk of the unknown. These motors were new and unproven. Factory owners would need to retrain maintenance staff, and shut down the factory for a moderate amount of time. It would entail a hefty capital expenditure for something whose benefits would only be seen in the long term, if at all. It seemed that a business wasn't going to die immediately just because it didn't switch from steam to electricity.

Over a few decades, however, things slowly changed. Factories with smaller power requirements made the leap first. Replacing smaller steam motors with smaller electrical motors brought the greatest gains, as electrical motors tended to be less powerful and the small steam engines were largely over-engineered and unnecessarily bulky. The world began to see change from the edges, small movements and cautious steps forward. Yet, by 1899, some 18 years after the introduction of the Edison Central Generating Station, still only 5 per cent of the power used in factories was electrically supplied (Clark, 1920).

Enter the group drive

It was the older and more traditional industries and factories that were the most reluctant to embrace the new technology. Newer industries with fewer or less strongly held preconceptions about what factories should look like adopted it most readily. This new form of production line propulsion really took off in the 1920s and 30s in those industries demonstrating rapid growth or necessitating new production processes like tobacco, fabricated metals and transportation, above all because they needed to increase the size of existing production units and construct new factories.

Competition in the design and development of electrical motors led to the equipment becoming smaller and cheaper, and gradually ingenuity was employed not just to change the propulsion mechanism, but to change the very layout of the factory.

In larger factories with vast power requirements, it seemed more sensible to split up the line drive shafts into smaller units, to group equipment in such a way so that machines that needed the same rotation speed, had the same operating hours and that would fit together sensibly should be placed in close proximity. Factory designers had once again based their thinking on what was known before – the concept of line drive shafts – and existing known techniques were adapted to incrementally improve them based on tried and tested methodology. This was known as 'group drive'.

The cost of modifying existing factories in this way was high, so this technique was initially only adopted in newly constructed factories. Rethinking things from blueprints made change far more economically viable. It also made more sense, because often these new production facilities were making more complex goods, had more detailed and varied needs, or required a wide range of speed control, including particularly precise speed control for sensitive operations such as wire drawing or hammering iron.

'Group drive' offered huge potential. Line drive systems serving the entire factory wasted about 40 per cent of the power generated due to their size. They allowed virtually no local control: if machines were to engage, disengage or use different speeds, a complex system of pulleys, levers to remove power connections and new belts would be needed, making the power even less efficient.

The first large-scale operation of group drive was the General Electric Company plant in Schenectady, New York, in the 1890s. Here 43 DC motors turned about 40 different line drive shafts. Large arrays of machines in proximity to each other could all be powered by a slightly smaller, local version of a line drive, each with its own electrical motor (Schurr *et al*, 1990).

Thinking driven by economists

In economic terms, the switch to group drive was easier to justify than building entirely new factories, since the existing line drive system would typically remain in situ as one of the components of the overall group drive. It was now possible to justify the capital expenditure as one that increased the total power capacity of the plant and explain this decision using this logic and mathematics. It worked psychologically too: nobody likes to buy something new with the implication that the previous purchase was a bad decision. The group drive system was a big success – by making motors smaller, and removing large amounts of millwork, factories saw decent leaps in improvement. These shorter drive systems produced far less friction, leading to energy savings. The risks of fire were somewhat reduced, and equipment could be arranged by the speed of rotation required so complex gear boxes and pulleys could be removed.

It was the apparent shift in thinking to group drive and the enthusiasm for this new way of thinking that arguably delayed the implementation of electricity even more. Group drive proved to be a distraction. It made factory managers content, it gave the illusion of great change, when, compared to what was actually possible, very little had happened. The resulting improvements removed any apparent dissatisfaction with the current situation and reduced the thirst to explore new avenues. If the electrification of line drives caused makers to sit back and feel proud that they'd done all they needed to, the creation of electrical group drives cemented this resting on laurels even further. It was felt that everything that could be done had been done.

So slowly and surely, as electrical motors became more efficient, cheap and durable, with more data-supported business cases, steam engines were slowly replaced. By 1920 the USA saw around 50 per cent of its power coming from electricity.

The real change: re-imagining factories around electricity

As is often the case, real change came about by several seemingly different movements coming together.

Electricity production got cheaper and far more reliable, and distribution improved slowly during the 1920s and 30s. It was now possible for factories to switch to electrical drive and not feel vulnerable without a back-up option. People recommending this change would be made to feel more confident, because the technology had evolved.

Electrical motors got cheaper and more efficient. Quite simply, years of refinement allowed motors to have lower running costs, with both parts and maintenance becoming cheaper, a greater labour pool to maintain the equipment was available, and the power per unit cost was much greater. Above all else, motors that were electrically driven became much smaller.

The demands of factories became more complex, as they moved away from linen-weaving to aircraft or complex consumer goods manufacture. This new demand was generated amongst a generation who now had electricity at home and who wanted electrical domestic goods.

When factories were built from scratch they were conceived and constructed in totally different ways than they would have been, had they been built on legacy water- or steam-powered operations. For the first time ever, rather than merely assuming that large drive shafts would be central to factory architectures and processes, designers worked around the machinery and the workflow that best suited the manufacturing process.

Factories were re-imagined. Everything known, assumed and fixed was challenged. Electricity meant that power effectively became pervasive: it became an easy thing, vital, transformative, it allowed new ways of considering energy, it afforded very new economics. New factories and designs could be constructed in the context of easy, fast, cheap, abundant energy, the electrical cables infinitely easier to manage than drive shafts.

Layouts of factories could follow the most sensible layouts for the manufacture of goods in the most efficient way. Huge productivity gains, visible from this one change, also reduced the messiness of the flow of goods in one go. Workers suddenly became both trained and empowered; they'd work harder and see the great effects of their responsibility. Factories could remove (or never build) the millwork. There could be windows, the fire risk was immediately reduced and ventilation improved. The notion of power or energy became not a physical element that drives the layout, but the background entity that makes anything possible. It was the enabler, not the constraint. Large gearboxes and pulleys were replaced with switches and rheostats.

Freed from the constraints that came from power distribution, activities on the factory floor could be reorganized to bring about much better production arrangements. Factories no longer needed to be elongated with complex flows; they could be any shape the company needed. Buildings could be constructed far more efficiently and multiple storeys were now possible. With equipment placed around the best possible flow of items through the factory, far higher productivity lowered the cost per unit of output.

The benefits of the new system were far-reaching and incredibly varied in nature. Factories suddenly became quieter. Long drive shafts had expanded and contracted with heat which led to endless vibrations that nearly deafened workers. Removing this system meant that factories became far quieter overnight.

Factories could now have far more open space; the buildings, now without the need to hold up heavy millwork, had more ventilation and natural light, with no dripping oil from overhead machinery.

There were no belts or pulleys overhead threatening to remove an arm with one false move. All these features meant better quality work drove higher quality and happier staff, who were now given more control over their output. They were trained to operate specific machines with more control and power to make decisions locally, they could start and stop things themselves, and not be reliant on being part of a bigger system.

More advanced machines were introduced, fabricating more intricate parts, thanks to the control and steadiness of motor power. The quality of goods rocketed.

But by far the biggest shift happened on a macro level. For hundreds of years the location of plants had been dictated by energy needs. At first the need was to locate near fast-running reliable water to power waterwheels, then it was the need to be near coal or near a transportation route that offered easy and cheap access to huge amounts of coal. Energy was never something that could be transported.

This requirement was completely removed by electricity, and for the first time in history factories were free. They could be near sources of employment in large cities, or they could be located near ports where inbound ingredients and products made from them could be transported far more freely.

The parallels here for modern working life are so clear. Even knowledge workers and those in contemporary industries have experienced little change in their working life since the advent of electricity. Companies' hierarchical structures, departmental silos, company office design, workflow processes have all changed little in the last 60 years. We've never truly embraced remote working, we've never rethought organizational design, even open-plan offices seem more about saving money than rethinking how best to get what is needed done. But we've far more to learn.

What can we learn from all this?

What we can learn from the very slow, very reluctant transformation around electricity is the following.

People think they've got it when they haven't

For nearly 40 years not only did very little really change, but for all that time, for all the annual meetings, the sales presentations, the consultants, the management theorists, the data, it appears every single person believed that they'd really understood the power of the change.

The period of incremental improvements wasn't lined with people complaining that progress wasn't fast enough. There was no movement demanding 'let's do more'. For several decades, everyone sat back pleased with what we'd done, which was simply to switch an old power mechanism for a new one. It was only in retrospect that we realized what mistakes we'd made.

This often seems the case with digitization. Grocery stores seem to think that by adding self-checkouts they've done enough; they don't think how technology could rewire their business fundamentally. Big-box retailers think that click-and-collect might be enough to stop the onslaught of Amazon. I sense banks see M-Pesa in Kenya as a curious case study and Venmo something that kids do, and that a nice new mobile banking app and a new-look website is really grasping the power of the new.

Companies need to realize that, so far, most of them have done nothing. They need to find these changes exciting, be enthralled to rethink their businesses around a whole toolkit of new possibilities, compare themselves not with how far they've come, but how much they could leapfrog into the future and over their competitors of today and tomorrow.

Economics gets in the way by not being imaginative enough

The chief financial officers (CFOs) and management consultants of the day were entirely wrong in how they thought about electricity. By thinking of electricity as a source of energy only, as merely a new way to power machines, the economists failed to understand the secondary benefits which were to really revolutionize lifestyle and open the door for new products and services.

Most businesses, like the factories of the past, are run with heavy influence (at the very least) from the company's financial leader.

Investment decisions in particular are based on complex accounting procedures where sunk costs, expected gains and time to pay back investments quite rightly lead the way. It's clear that in this time period, like today, accounting was done over a relatively short term. Nobody was looking at the payback over 60 years, but over the next 10 or so. Nobody was calculating the cost of not doing this and of competition unleashing this new power. Economics found old models with old assumptions and old limitations to evaluate the cost and benefit of the new, with no imagination for the benefits which were second order.

When factories were constructed *around* electricity and not as an *add-on*, some of the benefits were clear and predictable: the lower fire insurance, the cheaper energy costs, the savings on maintenance. But although predictable, many of these benefits couldn't easily be accounted for mathematically. What is the financial gain of quieter running conditions or having workers with fewer days off? What is the value of happier staff and more precisely made products?

And many benefits were totally impossible to foresee, particularly the second-order changes. Few people could have predicted that electricity would allow the displacement of factories closer to ports, or that brighter lighting would improve product inspection and raise quality.

Most accounting models are quite sensibly rational, but that doesn't mean everything that can be measured matters. Similarly, it doesn't mean that what can't fit into a spreadsheet doesn't have a financial implication, no matter how seemingly disconnected.

So, as your company looks to undertake change, be aware that transformational change is very hard to predict. The music industry was devoted to music being streamed but now treats most music as content marketing for the real money made in live concerts. The TV industry learned the wrong lesson from this and now drags its feet streaming programmes because it fails to see that when TV content is streamed, the potential arises to use personal data to make TV ads far more valuable. But this requires imagination beyond most financial thinkers. Few financial plans account for the cost of not doing anything. It may be that Ford would rather not make an electrically-driven car. It reduces their ability to make money in spare parts and maintenance, but they don't have that choice if Tesla and others create this market.

Muscle memory is strong: we apply the new to the old

When we face something new we find it hard to really rethink. We can't start with a blank sheet of paper; in order to feel more in control, we excitedly and rapidly attach it to what we understand.

We anchor it in processes, systems, infrastructure, assumptions of the past and use it like an oil to lubricate what we have. We don't notice we are doing it. Nobody sees how strange it is when digital watches in adverts show the time as 10:10 because that time looked good on an analogue watch. Few people notice how strange it is that their parents share one e-mail address because a postal address was one single address for everyone.

Companies use computer systems where you typically look up people by their postal address because that's what systems in the past used, when today people are far more likely to move home than change their mobile phone number or their e-mail address – but no system has yet been designed by taking this into account.

Companies today need to be wary of the assumptions they make and the baggage they carry from the past. Retailers always needed to hold inventory of what they sold; now they can be a storefront for anyone's product. In fact, if you have an audience, anyone today can become a retailer in seconds. They just become the shop window for someone else to fulfil. Turo shows you can be a car rental company and not own cars. Airbnb shows that, with little work, you can go from providing accommodation to providing experiences. As you think about the future, be careful that assumed needs do not limit you. Does a bank need branches today? Do you need to own things? Do you need staff or can you outsource? Should you really be structured like your competitors or around what people want?

Change needs to be deep

As I will cover in the next few chapters, profound changes in technology require equally profound shifts in how we think. Such fundamental changes require us to rethink even the most core elements of what we do. To simply augment or embellish is to misunderstand what transformation is possible. If businesses had been more positive about the power of the new, if, instead of trying to simply digest the possibilities, they'd spent time expanding upon them, life would have changed more quickly.

By bolting on the new to the edge, we do what's easiest and requires least change. It's quickest and takes the least effort. Who wants to make a new process chart when you can just keep everything where it is? But as I'll explore later, the change needs to come from the core, not the edge.

No foresight on things that have never happened before

It wasn't that company owners could see the potential of electricity and made decisions based on this foresight. Rather, they couldn't imagine something that had never existed before. No rational, reasonable, engineering-led, output-focused, mathematically-driven person could ever have foreseen what electricity meant. Teams needed diverse talent, dreamers, thinkers, creative types to really see the impact that the second- and third-order changes and implications would mean.

Technology is background not foreground

It is people, not technology, who transform business. While it's easy to think that all the changes enabled by electricity were brought about by the technology, they were actually driven by people. It was the people who worked in factories who could now see products better in sunlight, who worked harder because they had more control, who spent less time moving products in inefficient ways, or commuting to work. It was people whose health improved, who worked in safer and less noisy conditions. In every single technological shift, technology is always essential, but more often than not, it's really about people: workers, customers, salespeople or marketing folk. Empathy to what is needed is as, if not more, essential than the understanding of complex technology. More than anything else we see people want solutions not technology. We have to focus much more on better ways to do things, or making things in new ways, not on the technology itself.

A mid-stage often exists

The group line drive provides a good framework to see what happens when a way of thinking is bold enough to challenge what has been done before, but not determined, imaginative or deep enough to really make a difference. While it's easy to look back at the section about group drive and see merit in the change it brought, it's also possible to see it as a delaying factor in allowing proper change to happen. This was an incremental improvement to an old way of doing things. It was change that was buyable and makeable. It was comfortable and had the illusion of making all the difference that was possible. It's these seemingly big, but in retrospect tiny, changes that often get in the way of true innovation, as we will discuss later. We see from the group drive and from the early stages of domestic electricity, the battles between AC and DC systems and the closed proprietary nature of early home power systems, that often life gets more complex before it gets simpler.

Timing is vital

Being a factory owner in an age when things change fast was hard. Power generation costs came down fast, as did the cost of the motors themselves, the number of experts who could electrify factories increased and the costs of retrofitting also came down. In 20:20 retrospective vision, it's pretty easy to map out what companies should have done and when, but at the time knowing what to shift to and when must have been extremely difficult. As we venture around the planet and see companies laying fibre-optic cables to supply ultra-fast internet, we wonder if maybe they should have waited for 5G networks and not dug up streets. When we see aircraft with large seat-back screens, it's interesting to consider, since we've now got phones and tablets, whether they should have just spent the money on excellent Wi-Fi instead. Should we be constructing high-speed trains or waiting for the Hyperloop? Should we embark on using early artificial intelligence (AI) in our business now or wait until it improves and work around a better core system?

It's companies that are newly built for the age that unleash the real power

A combination of all of the above factors meant that it wasn't the existing factories that used the new technology first. Yet I think the biggest factor was something else: the sunk costs and mental entrenchment of old factory owners.

If you are running a successful textile mill and your company has been growing for 40 years, with a factory that appears to work just fine, you would be unlikely to suddenly wake up one day and sink vast amounts of money into changing. Even though things can break down, you've had decades of experience with your system and equipment. You'd be more comfortable making smaller changes in an existing system than throwing out everything and starting again. It would take a disastrous loss of income to even contemplate this. This loss of income would only happen if and when another factory, in direct competition with your product, moved forward with changes, overtaking you and producing better products. It would take decades for this to happen and when you finally realized it was happening, it would be too late.

As a result of this reluctance to change, it wasn't the old textile plants or established and profitable businesses that led the change with unit power; it was the newer, smaller companies that were hungrier for success. Companies building things that had never been made before – planes, fridges, cigarettes – led the way.

As you consider the status quo and your business today, it's easy to see the reason why you've not changed. Like the apocryphal frog who boils to death, you are perhaps now warm and more relaxed than ever. Perhaps it's too late to muster the energy to jump and harder than ever to make that happen – which scarily is what you need to do most.

Business owners tell themselves lies all the time to feel comfortable. People will always want to touch things before they buy, people won't pay for news, people always need X, competitor Y is different because they are online, we know our customers better, we have better relationships with our suppliers… the list goes on.

Yet maybe you are just comforting yourself, maybe you are merely understanding the world in a way that suits you, a way that requires the least risk and change. It could be that you need to make huge alterations and that the time to act is now. As Amara's Law states, people often overestimate the amount of change over the short term and underestimate it over the long term, but I also think they underestimate the depth to which the most meaningful technology needs to be applied (Amara, 2006). First, we shape our tools, then they shape us – this is thinking from John Culkin, (although it has been widely attributed to Marshall McLuhan) on which we don't ponder enough (Culkin, 1967).

It's more helpful to assume that everything will change rather than to underestimate it

After the banking crash in 2006, governments around the world pumped over $12 trillion into the economy and quickly. They did so because they felt it was better to do too much and too soon, than too little too late. Similarly, when it comes to business planning and transformation, it's better to apply more imagination to the future, to look further ahead, to overestimate the changes in the world, than it is to presume things won't alter.

I'm sure it's clear by now that the missteps we took with the electrical age provide the perfect lens through which to view our mistakes with the transformation to digital. Every aspect and lesson learned has a parallel in the modern world. How we only applied the new technology to the edges, not the core. How accounting processes diminished its value, and factory owners refused to invest enough, assuming they could ride it out. How, in domestic applications, people could not really see the benefit, and how companies created closed systems out of protectionism. We see that what really changes isn't the technology itself but the systems, appliances, ways of working that are built on top of this new world. Profound technology creates existential change. It rewires everything. It's wiser to assume that everything will change rather than to underestimate it. The next chapter will explore how new technology arrives, what it looks like and what to do about it.

So, as we seek to establish how best to apply new technology, it's clear we must understand not just the technology itself, but its meaning. We need to look at the ways technology has effected change before.

References

Amara, R (2006) available at: http://www.oxfordreference.com/view/
10.1093/acref/9780191826719.001.0001/q-oro-ed4-00018679

Clark, J A (1920) cited in The 1920s (1920–1929), *EC&M*, 01/06,
available from: http://www.ecmweb.com/content/1920s-1920-1929
[last accessed 7 December 2017]

Culkin, J M (1967) A schoolman's guide to Marshall McLuhan, *Saturday
Review,* pp51–70

Schurr, S H, Burwell, C C, Devine, W D and Sonenblum, S (1990)
Electricity in the American Economy: Agent of technological progress,
Praeger, New York City

Schwartz, E (2012) We're using way more paper than we have before,
Gizmodo, 3 April, available from: https://gizmodo.com/5898830/were-
using-way-more-paper-than-we-ever-have-before [last accessed
7 December 2017]

The Victorian Emporium (2011) History of Lighting, 30 May, available
from: https://www.thevictorianemporium.com/publications/history/
article/history_of_lighting [last accessed 7 December 2017]

03
The three eras of technology

We've seen how last century the world collectively got the meaning of electricity wrong. Taking a look at this century allows us to learn even more lessons from other and more recent examples. It is by studying how technology is adopted, how companies and society respond and when, how and where change should be applied, that we can best harness the potential of technology and establish when and how to do so.

In this chapter we will investigate the adoption process and the notion of three eras: the three distinct stages in the adoption of any technology. I hope that by understanding the concepts we can become more confident in how, when and where to apply change. In this chapter I will be establishing patterns that we can use to make sense of change, to become more confident and to paint a more optimistic vision that we can embrace.

For all the progress made in the digital age – our lives embellished by smartphones, TV shows beamed on demand, online retailers, all the services we can now access directly by ourselves – and for all the robot-centred auto-plants and the levering of new management techniques that best utilize these new forces, it's not immediately obvious that productivity has been drastically changed by the 'digital revolution'. Of course, productivity per worker goes up per year, but there is no drastic change of gradient, as is illustrated in Figure 3.1. How can this be?

Figure 3.1 US productivity per worker in real GDP: quarterly from Q1 1947 to Q2 2016

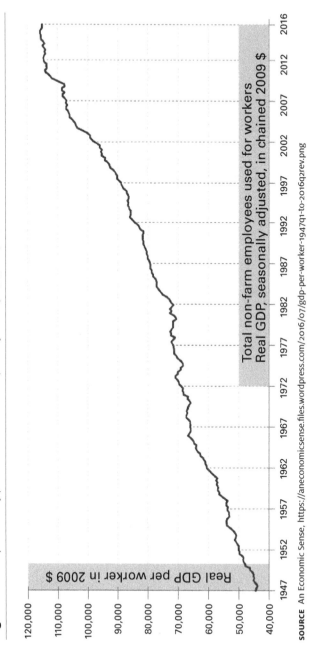

SOURCE An Economic Sense, https://aneconomicsense.files.wordpress.com/2016/07/gdp-per-worker-1947q1-to-2016q2rev.png

The three phases

The lack of change in productivity has been seen before. As we've learned from the introduction and use of electricity in the Industrial Revolution, there are three phases to the uptake of technology:

1 First, we have a pre-technology environment, before the new technology is discovered or used in any way. In this period things generally are understood, the pace of change is slow and improvements are incremental.

2 Then a new technology or way of thinking with the potential to change everything is installed or disseminated. This happens around existing mindsets and processes, augmenting and lubricating what went before. At this stage we have both the new and the old, with competing systems, inherited protocols, the feeling of change and panic, and where we often live with the most confusion and uncertainty.

3 And then we have a third phase where we make sense of the new technology, where systems are rebuilt for the new world. It is in this final stage, when society and the commercial world appear to have made sense of the change, that the technology moves to the background and is widely understood and built upon. It's this final stage where things appear simply to work.

Often things appear to get more complex before they get simple. Nearly everyone likely to read this book in 2018 will have electrical power at their fingertips and around them. Power is abundant, reliable, relatively cheap and simple. Apart from strange plugs around the world (increasingly standardized as USB plugs), it seems to be uniform and straightforward. As a result, we don't think about power because it works.

We once noticed computers a lot. We had Macs that didn't work with PCs. We had prompts to load computer programs, machines would run out of storage, they'd crash *all the time*. At university, computers were all kept in a special room. Computers were new, scarce, exciting, you'd most likely have to wait to get on one. I remember the first machine at school with a hard drive. I didn't get how it could just have all the programs in it already; it was magical.

For many years we'd notice how many of our possessions had a power supply, we'd note the things that had 'computers inside', but now we don't. We used to turn TVs on and off, and shut down PCs. Everything had a prominent on/off switch. Today we rarely bother. It's even hard to define what is and what isn't a computer. A tablet is a computer, but is Amazon Echo? Is a Google Wi-Fi router a computer? Is a Sonos speaker? My TV may or may not have a processor: it's not important to me. Everything is just increasingly smart.

When you think about a technology, when you notice it, it's a sign it's not yet working perfectly. It's rather paradoxical that what you notice least is often what works best. The fact you get angry when your phone isn't rendering movies immediately is a testament to your expectations that it should always be perfect. It's with this thought that we can see we are post-electricity and post-computerization, but now we are in the midst of the most complicated part of the digital age.

The pre-electricity age

For millennia, we lived in the pre-electricity age. Either we had no power and no factories or, as we started constructing them in the early Industrial Revolution, factories relied on water or steam for power. The location and design of these factories and the manufacturing processes used within them all evolved over time. Progress was relatively straightforward, change was slow, and increasingly focused. Lubrication technology may have made line drives a little more efficient, new materials made pulleys better, gear boxes gave more control over speed, steam plants got more powerful, but all the changes were designed to optimize existing equipment and processes within a pretty fixed environment.

The domestic environment was also one of relatively limited change. Houses at the time were focused on better provision of running water and reducing the risk of disease through improved sanitation. It was an era of incremental improvements in heating technology, from open fires to wooden stoves. Another focus was on how to reduce the risk of fire or how better to respond to fire risk. Before the vast changes that would occur as electricity spread through the world, life was simple: there were no compatibility issues between windmills and waterwheels, there was no chaos as people switched from horses to oxen to draw their ploughs. No management consultants would swoop in to tell roof thatchers about Six Sigma hay. In short, in retrospect it was a time of slow change, agreement on how to optimize towards a better solution, regardless of how it may have felt at the time.

The mid-electricity age

The discovery of electricity and the ability to harness its power, both in its generation and transmission, and the ability to use it, had enormous effects in virtually every direction. It was a time of great change, complexity, chaos and vast disagreements.

For a long middle stage, people lived in a hybrid age: a pre-electricity world which was being adapted at the edge, and with minimal effort, for the electrical age. Throughout this period, we had pre-electrical thinking and constructs running in parallel at the same time with electrically-altered businesses and processes.

In business and factories, there was a spectrum of companies operating with electricity being used in vastly different ways. Some businesses changed nothing, stubbornly refusing to see any benefit. Others made tiny changes, alterations at the periphery of what was done before. Yet others made larger changes, embracing the potential of what was possible, but – rather like electric group drive – did so with limited imagination and investment. And we had the beginnings of pure-play 'electrical' companies: businesses built for the modern age, founded conceptually and operationally on the new source of power.

During this period there was mass confusion, little agreement and many choices. There was no best practice, but unproven mathematics and new theories abounded. The confusion led to the creation of consultants. The first recognized management consulting firm was formed in 1890 by Arthur D Little, initially specializing in technical research, later building a specialism in what became known as 'management engineering', then evolving into management consultants as we know them today. Companies employed specialist and well-paid staff to assess the potential impact of electricity and then to drive business transformation with it.

It was a time of great uncertainty and non-standardization, requiring new regulations, agreements and protocols in order to best harness the potential of power.

In the UK, The Electricity Supply Act of 1926 led to the setting up of the National Grid to standardize the nation's electricity supply and established the first synchronized AC grid. Yet for a long time, because it was new, confusing and misunderstood, electricity wasn't deemed particularly important. A bit like the internet today, which is still largely regarded as a nice thing to have and not a human right, it wasn't until 1934 that the Public Utility Holding Company Act recognized electricity utilities as public goods of importance along with gas, water, and telephone companies, outlining restrictions and providing regulatory oversight of their operations.

As discussed in Chapter 2, in homes, schools, universities, healthcare and many other areas, electricity led to a proliferation of new appliances, new ways to live life, new ways to think about the world and women entering the workforce. It was a time of great debate about the changing nature of society, of gender role models, a time of big philosophical questions about the nature of humanity, of resistance to change and desire to resort to simpler times. There were fears of mass job losses and protesting workers, and the birth of the Arts and Crafts movement as a rebellion against the sweeping standardization and loss of artisanal practices. There were whole periods where the new technology felt disruptive beyond any good it could ever bring. There were massive increases in wealth for those who took advantage, huge changes to social fabric and the value and meaning of work – and two world wars!

It was while this new technology was being unequally adopted and unfairly distributed geographically, demographically and culturally, that we talked most about the implications of these changes. And it happened over a long period of time, as electricity spread around the world, and moved to developing nations, to different sectors and different use cases. Figure 3.2 shows the n-gram trend lines of references to electrification in books in the English language corpus. It is obvious that it became a big topic of conversation from

Figure 3.2 Frequency of the term 'electrification' in the English language corpus, 1800–2000

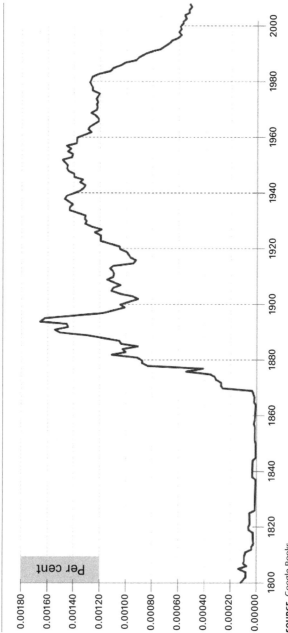

SOURCE Google Books

1870 onwards, before taking over 100 years to become something we didn't notice, think about, discuss or work around.

The post-electricity age

Postmodernism in architecture was a movement started by a generation of designers who had grown up with modernist architecture. They were so close and comfortable with it, it was so ingrained and natural to them, that they didn't need to play by its rules. They didn't need to signal to others that they understood it; it was just known that they got it. This confidence and innate understanding of modernism allowed them to playfully, confidently and knowingly design a world that could move past it. So, when I use the term 'post' in this chapter I'm talking about the same idea: a group of people or a society having the confidence and the maturity to accept the idea of moving forward, creating new things in the world, and then collectively looking back on our progress.

Electricity had the same watershed moment as architecture. Many years after the arrival of electricity we got to a place where electricity wasn't a thing. It wasn't there to be designed for. It wasn't simply 'not new' – it was a given. There was no celebration of it. Like oxygen it was just the natural order of life. There was no one set moment, no stories in the press, no anniversary we now celebrate; we got to the point where it became notable by its absence.

A technology is truly here when it fits into the background. We usually think that those growing up with a technology, who embrace it naturally and understand it innately, are 'natives'. But the people of today are not 'electricity natives': we are beyond that. The world today just makes sense in the era of electricity. We don't see companies struggling to adapt, we don't talk of 'heads of electricity' as we talk about 'heads of finance', we don't define companies on the stock market as being electricity-centric. There are no topics of contention, no new standards being launched, no legal cases rooted in the awkwardness of what this new power means. Things are very simple now. There is no duplicity, we don't own both electricity- and steam-driven appliances. We've made it. We now live firmly in the post-electricity age.

The three-era thinking has been borne out by other technologies. Another good example of this same pattern is computerization, which happened between the early 1970s and the late 2000s.

The pre-computer age

Before the mainframe and then personal computers, life across business, education, home and transportation was largely settled in the post-electricity age. Progress again was generally simple, convergent, and without controversy. Management consultants worked with factories to increase efficiencies, new theories like Just-in-Time manufacturing and Six Sigma were introduced and then perfected. When you look back at this time, it seems amazing. People on trains taking briefcases to work, the use of Xerography machines not printers, people around the world making phone calls (and from desks!), calendars on paper. In this era, offices were aligned like command and control systems replicated from the armed forces with a strict organizational hierarchy, an essential structure when communication takes time and costs money.

Business in this age consisted of forms to fill in, stamping stamps and internal mail protocols. Progress was slow and improvements limited: slightly faster photocopiers, cheaper ink, better workflows, cheaper and more advanced calculators developed at snail's pace. Desks were lined with intrays and outboxes. There we no blue screens of death, no 'systems down for maintenance' at weekends, no server issues or hacking scandals. No computer rooms, no IT support function. I'm certainly not suggesting life was better, but everything worked smoothly and slowly. Life was simple and effective, and about to undergo a huge shift.

The mid-computer age

The advent of computers didn't change business overnight. As with electricity, it took a while, was ignored by many businesses, and adopted with different speeds, enthusiasm and depth by different companies, sectors and nations. It was perhaps partly because of this asymmetry that things felt very complex.

For this age, new skills were required, new equipment needed to be purchased and new systems created. We first used them to embellish the existing structures and systems. We bolted on a new IT department, reluctantly and entirely as a support function. In the beginning we needed computers to fit around us, but then we needed to change around them.

What changed was largely an addition to rather than a replacement for what we had in the past. Initially, we still held briefcases and kept paper calendars. We printed out e-mails, and we kept internal mail. Over time people talked about workflow management in new ways. Mail became electronic, we invited people to meetings with digital calendars (which some people have still not adopted!), we used intranets, and laptops allowed people to work from home and stay connected. Then things again got overwhelmingly complex. We had mixed protocols with Mac vs PC, and different types of printer (remember daisywheel printers?!). The systems of the old were supplanted by the new, not rethought. It was painful. In fact, the only thing harder than changing technology is changing the way that people use it. IT departments to this day have an expression PICNIC, which stands for Problem In Chair, Not In Computer to convey the degree to which it is the people who are lagging behind.

Faced with complexity and new things to learn, we replicated the familiar units of the past. We took all the old-world systems and digitized them. Skeuomorphism, the design concept of making digital items resemble their real-world counterparts, was a way to aid the transition into the new era. Mail became e-mail, with 'addresses' and inboxes. We made 'folders' and 'trash' and 'desktops' as digital equivalents. PowerPoint had 'slides' like early slide projectors and floppy disks represented 'saving', which is wonderfully anachronistic, as is 'return' which stands for 'carriage return' from typewriters – and don't even start me on 'cc' for carbon copy.

Slowly new things were made, retailers used barcodes to allow better stock-keeping and make checkouts slower and then faster as people adapted. These changing, uncertain times proved to be incredibly profitable times for management consultancies and experts. The extremely potent power of computers was clear to see, but advice was essential.

Figure 3.3 Capital investment from companies in hardware and software

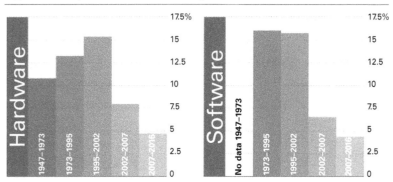

SOURCE Economic Policy Institute, http://www.epi.org/publication/robots-or-automation-are-not-the-problem-too-little-worker-power-is/?utm_content=buffer27c7b&utm_medium=social&utm_source=twitter.com&utm_campaign=buffer

Questions kept business leaders awake at night: what new equipment, staff and training were needed, what did it really mean for individual businesses, and what could be outsourced? It's while advising people in the moments of greatest change, deepest complexity and most potential and fear that consultants can both charge the most and create such valuable advantages. As illustrated in Figure 3.3, it was at this time that companies invested the most in new hardware and software to best adapt to this change, reaching a peak in the period 1973 to 2002.

Yet at the same time, businesses mainly stuck to the order and methodologies of the past. Cloud computing didn't necessarily lead to the era of working remotely. Extra computing power didn't necessarily mean schools used digital whiteboards. We didn't use less paper and the paperless office of the future never appeared. Instead we had a parallel life. In this mid-computing age, computers were most visible. Universities and schools had big computer rooms, the newness was gathered in a place and almost shown off.

The post-computer age

While we still suffer things that don't work, fill in an inordinate amount of forms by hand and await the paperless office, we're now ostensibly in the post-computer age. You don't see many retailers who don't scan items and automatically link them to inventories, or office workers carrying briefcases, or calculators on many desks. Things generally work: even my Mac will talk to my PC, they both use Google Drive and the internet has been the glue. The computing power behind what we do has been all but forgotten about.

Today no management consultants talk about computerization strategies, no companies have people tasked with adding computing power to businesses. The very role of IT has gone from the job of the future to a support function, maintaining, not building. We don't have conferences about 'unleashing the power of computers'; it's just known to be part of the foundational elements of the world in which we live. Figure 3.4 showcases the drop in the use of the term 'computerization' in English language books from 1800 to 2000, illustrating how it took off in the 1960s then gradually faded away from our collective consciousness.

Of course we could use computers better, but the focus now is increasingly on the connectivity of the devices we use, on the automation made possible by data sharing and processing, all of which is more about the next era: the digital age.

The shortening cycles

At this point it is important to note the change in pace which characterizes the adoption of new technologies. Many theorists talk about the four 'Industrial Revolutions'. And while the descriptions and starting points of each one varies between proponents, one change is impossible to go unnoticed – the speed at which these cycles commence and terminate:

- *The first revolution*: the arrival of water and steam power as well as the creation of huge factories and industrial production happened over a period of around 100 years.

- *The second revolution*: the uptake of electricity and the creation of new appliances based on electricity took around 50 years.

- *The third revolution*: the last revolution to be completed, the use of computing and automation to increase productivity, took perhaps 25 years for the world to fully embrace.

Figure 3.4 Frequency of the term 'computerization' in the English language corpus, 1800–2000

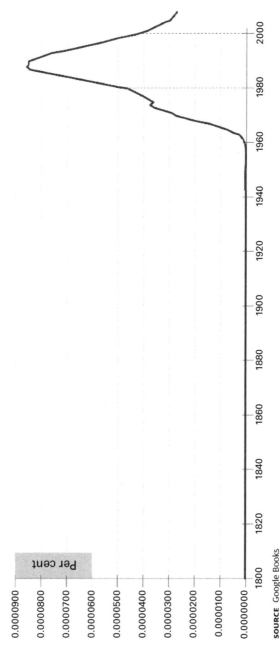

source Google Books

Today we live in a post-electrical, post-computerized age. We don't reflect on how many hours a day we use power, we don't think of what appliances are electric, or how many have chips in them, but we probably do know which and how many items are connected to the internet. Let's explore what is happening in the current revolution:

- *The fourth revolution*: the digital and connected age.

The pre-digital age

Remember an age where devices had just one function? It was when media was physical, and when technologies lived alongside and in parallel to each other, but rarely intertwined. Retail was either in-store or via mail-order home shopping, or if you were impatient, the phone. 'Dial now, if operators are busy, do try later' and 'please allow six to eight weeks for delivery'.

Media channels were labelled after the singular device we consumed them on: TVs, newspapers, magazines, radio. There was no confusion or overlap. You wouldn't see content on a TV that then couldn't play in your region. Banknotes and coins were our primary way to spend money in the world. We had credit cards too, the 'shunk shunk' of carbon paper, and cheque books, a sort of IOU note that people took seriously. But our use of technology wasn't messy.

It may not have seemed like it at the time, but in retrospect, life was simple. Progress was steady but largely linear. Of course, things changed: we moved from VHS to DVD; cassettes fell aside as the compact disc took over. Mail-order shopping got a bit better, but was still essentially 100 years old. The changes were small. They didn't change the retail landscape or logistics supply chain. There were no software updates to get headphones to work, a light switch didn't need a firmware flash, in a world with no connectivity your toaster didn't stop talking to your kettle because it never started to. There were no terms and conditions to start using your oven.

We cared about what pictures we took because we could only take as many as the films we carried could store, and getting them printed, the only way to see what we took, was expensive and took time. It was a land of the physical. Cars were chosen on how they looked, how they handled the road, how they were made. Specifications and improvements were very tactile: a better TV was a bigger TV with a crisper picture. Better loudspeakers could go louder and be a bit more bassy. As things got older, from radios to cars to cameras, things got worn out, and worse, cassettes got mangled, CDs scratched. This was life in the analogue age.

We owned a lot of things, but we had to. Without a camera you couldn't take pictures, without a TV you couldn't watch anything, without a radio you got no local news. While we spent a lot of our disposable income on things, it never seemed extravagant. Overlaps were small so the benefit each device brought was simple and clear.

The mid-digital age

At first, the pre-digital age evolved slowly. Products became digitized. Photos became bits. Knowledge moved from volumes of encyclopedias to Encarta on a CD (or 20). At first the change wasn't great. While CDs were technically digital, they felt physical in nature. Renting a DVD wasn't a different behaviour to renting a VHS tape. We still lived in an era of limited choice of most things, of geography being key to retail, of distribution being a key cost.

The internet started to change things, but we still looked through the past in the rear-view mirror. The phone book became an online directory. Printed magazines became websites. Newspapers became 'digital paper' versions of what we knew, and we placed the same content 'online'.

The connected world has made everything more complex and created challenges. Now that music or video is merely data on a server, not a CD that you touch, it makes it harder to charge money for it, which has destroyed entire manufacturing, distribution and retail industries. Now flights or hotels, insurance policies and pretty much everything we can own can be compared online. It has suddenly killed smaller outfits and created an open, global marketplace in which the former information asymmetries which enabled businesses to make a profit no longer exist. The mid-digital age has seen the role of many companies vanish, especially middle layers in processes. Why do we need department stores, talent agents, record labels, travel agents, insurance brokers? It makes no sense. A lot of destruction has been felt. Blockbusters was killed by Netflix. Despite inventing digital photography, Kodak lost its way, and Nokia moved to irrelevance despite pioneering the smartphone. Coming first and being a pioneer has not been kind to companies in this era. There is much confusion and uncertainty. Newspapers and magazines face the toughest challenges; they find it harder to make money from advertising online, but dare not place content behind paywalls, when people expect everything for free.

The early stages of the internet have been brutal for many. We've collectively failed to find ways to build value. We exist amidst the foundations, the principles and the built environment of the pre-digital world, embellished only by the potential of what's next. We take the thinking of the past, and cram it into containers of the future, where it just doesn't fit. It's a nightmare for incumbent companies, for brands, for regulators, but a wonderful time for lawyers and consultants.

I call this 'peak complexity'. We are in the mid-digital age. This energy – the disruptive forces, the vast feeling of change, the acceleration of complexity, the stress of companies fighting for the profit margins of the past – is where we now lie. The complexity is found in every aspect of our lives and we tend not to notice it because we're enamoured by the wonder of the new.

In 2005 I would wake up to perhaps 50 e-mails and 3 texts. I had a personal e-mail, a work e-mail and one phone. Today, as form follows funding, all apps grow towards the sun that is monetization and they all offer messaging. We now have the same number of people to reach, but messages to check on Yammer, Dropbox, Slack and 45 other inboxes. We have to think not of who we want to chat to but how. Cognitive burden is rife in this age, as are the lost opportunities. The BBC won't play any content outside the UK because global usage rights have not been cleared, despite the internet being popular for over 10 years.

Payment systems don't make sense. If you jump in any taxi in any city and ask if they take credit cards, they either scoff 'of course yes', or 'heck no'. You can only pay with cash (not cards) on American

Eagle (American Airlines' regional brand) flights, but can only pay with cards (and not cash) on American Airlines flights. You can authorize a payment with 30,000 data points on your fingerprint with Touch ID, but then need to squiggle a pen on a paper receipt to combat fraud. It's a time where the teething problems of digitalization and the battles for territory define our experience. Facebook want to keep you in their app, Amazon Echo doesn't want to show YouTube, Google Home won't play nicely with Apple. Some retailers won't accept the collection or return of online goods in real stores. At other stores, if you want to know if they have an item in stock, they may have to make phone calls to each branch.

More than anything we have the wonderful and amazing promise of the new built on the foundations of the past. Websites that at first look amazing but within four clicks lead you to an old back end system they hoped you'd never find. Amazing mobile apps for companies, clearly designed by better teams and with more money than was available for the clunky website. Airlines that offer pilots iPads to speed up paperwork, but still need dot-matrix printouts on blue computer paper of the manifest paperwork. It's a time when the very concept of TV channels and electronic programming guides make no sense: the two least important things to most young people are the company that commission the show and when it is broadcast – the two dimensions used to navigate your way round TV shows.

What binds all these lacklustre experiences and all the perceived errors together, and what more positively shows the way into the future, is that, so far, we've translated pre-digital thinking and pulled it through a digital lens. We've taken every behaviour, product or physical item and changed it remarkably very little. We rechannel the old through the new, we merely pull the old stuff through new frames, never rethinking what is possible. The first radio shows were readings from newspapers, early TV shows were just plays with cameras pointed at them, early websites were digitized newspapers. In fact much of the modern world, when looked at critically, seems amazingly unchanged. Everything we see today is a mere iteration of the past, incremental improvements of the old with added technology.

It explains why online shopping appears both brand new, innovative and slick, but happens to mirror the exact same choice and design architecture from catalogues from a bygone age. We see catalogue shopping of the 1960s but with a website and e-mail functionality. It is so exciting to think of what we can do if we dare to work around what technology can now enable. How can we rethink online shopping? What can car insurance become? How can people pay for things most easily? These are wonderful times to be in business.

It's in this era that companies hire 'digital heads' to champion new thinking and new technology, in order to answer some of these questions. We witness this in the endless articles, the trending topics, the hashtags about disruption, the plethora of conferences.

The post-digital age

The first internet era: digitizing interfaces that already existed (catalogues newspapers). Now: creating the ones that should have existed.
LEVIE, 2014

Apple's new recently launched Face ID system uses a camera to capture accurate face data by projecting and analysing over 30,000 invisible dots on your face. It automatically adapts to changes in your appearance, like wearing make-up or growing facial hair. It's pretty advanced stuff.

At the same time, and seemingly unrelated, at this moment the USA is considering building a wall for about $50 billion to keep some people out because it cares that much about security. In order to get back into the USA, or the UK or any other nation, you need to hand over a piece of paper, a passport, which may or may not have a microchip in it. A port-of-entry official will look at you, and establish if you are that person. The entire current global movement of people system, costing hundreds of billions of dollars per year, is rooted in people looking a bit like their picture, carrying around paper booklets, visiting embassies to get other bits of paper put in them, which are then stamped with rubber stamps and ink.

I don't know if this astounds you, but it seems a bit strange to me. It would be interesting to imagine a system whereby we record people's faces, have a global database, have visas as digital permissions stored centrally, and never require anyone to carry a passport. It is terrifying to many to imagine this (and the role of privacy in the future is explored later in this book), but it's hard to see us having more privacy as the world moves forward and it's interesting to consider what benefits this can bring. It would be fun to consider this: what if we didn't have boarding passes as digital equivalents of paper boarding passes, but we could board a plane with nothing but our face? Or we never needed to carry a credit card, because our payment was linked to our face or fingerprint? We've tended to add digital thinking on top of antiquated devices, paper tickets, passports, boarding passes, rather than rethink systems from new.

We keep making these mistakes. We keep adding technology to broken systems. It's not hard for a bank to realize cheques are a pain in the neck to deposit and to make a cheque scanning app, but it's thinking about technology the wrong way. We make robots that can do bricklaying, but shouldn't we be thinking of entirely new construction methods? This all goes to show that it's rethinking the process that's hard. What needs to change is the underlying system.

In this post-digital age, we will think about *people* in the age of technology, not the technology itself. We will reinvent physical retail because online behaviours mean we now expect to find things fast, see items that go alongside them and never have to queue to pay.

We will make better products that do more than the sum of its parts, like the Nest thermostat – not just the first thermostat that you can program without a computer science degree, but a thermostat that learns and makes your home more efficient, without you doing anything.

The post-digital age will be amazing. Like pre-digital, nobody will think of 'digital' in this age. The concept will move into the background and, much like oxygen or electricity, we'll understand digital to be transformative yet irrelevant. There will be no more 'chief digital officers' in the same way that a 'chief electricity officer' doesn't exist today.

In the post-digital age, digital technology will be a vast, quiet element forming the seamless backbone of life. The internet will be a background utility, noticeable only by its absence. Smart homes will work. Video will follow us around. Content will be paid for... all seamlessly and effortlessly.

We will no longer talk of TV vs online, or mobile vs desktop. Retailers won't consider online vs physical as a division worthy of note; they will just celebrate sales. Advertising will work around people, seamlessly telling sequential stories to move people to purchase. Content won't care about national boundaries; even contemporary notions like currency or language will become less central to life.

In the post-digital age, maybe we won't build libraries to access books, maybe we'll establish that we should ensure everyone has a smartphone. Maybe we'll vote securely and immediately and for virtually no cost on key issues of governance like welfare payments or health details.

People will be born truly digitally native. Parents won't feel as anxious as they currently do about their children using these technologies. Kids will instinctively use them as babies, and continue to develop and nurture them as they grow alongside technology. Perhaps the most blurred line will be that between the real and the virtual. Our sense of reality, of time and place, will be the most complex for us to understand.

How can businesses leverage the power of the post-digital age?

Wake up, get excited, change

Let's get over ourselves. The internet and the smart are not remotely new. We kid ourselves that we've not yet got to grips with them because it's all happened so fast. Retailers who have yet to embrace PayPal or Apple Pay or Klarna, apps that fail to use Touch ID to log in, companies that don't use e-mail to allow customers to reach them – come on everyone, hurry up. Nor do I think companies show any sign of being excited about new technology; they drag their feet. I don't see that companies understand how much this matters. If banks for years were constructed of fine marble and over-engineered with large Doric pillars, how have they not understood that their digital touchpoints reflect their identity in the same way? Most banks' digital presence offers the same reassurance as a bank operating in a port-a-cabin in a car park in the middle of a wasteland.

Make things simple

We often seem drawn to do and want everything that is new. Companies want to show to the world they get virtual reality, so make a VR experience. They need to show trade magazines they are quick to adopt chatbots, they want to have a 3D printer in a store, create dynamically rendered and personalized advertising. But do consumers care? Does it make a difference to them? In complex times people seek simplicity. If your airline app that tells people when the plane is boarding works 90 per cent of the time, knowing you will only miss 1 in 10 flights isn't comforting; it's worse than useless. If you are Apple, don't make a laptop that offers the wonder of a USB-C connection, but won't somehow let you charge your phone without an expensive dongle. Be considerate. In times of peak complexity, be mindful enough to consider the customer's viewpoint. Make simple things well. Say no to everything that doesn't demonstrably help people. Don't over-promise, manage expectations, make things that just work.

Build around the possibilities, not around the past

The main lesson from what we've seen is the degree to which our muscle memory relies so heavily on the past. The first steamships had masts for sails because that's what ships looked like. The first horseless carriages looked the same as horse-drawn carriages because that's what fabricators knew how to make. The first advertising for digital watches displayed the same time as 10:10 because that's what looked most attractive on analogue faces and hands. It is amazing how frequently we build on what's been done before without rethinking.

Imagine if someone in the 1900s, seeing a horse-drawn carriage and fully aware of motors, transmission systems, combustion engines and more advanced machinery thought there was a better way. Imagine they sought to make a better version with their knowledge, but no imagination. They wouldn't change the form of the vehicle, they'd forge a hugely advanced form of animatronic horse that pulled the vehicle. It would be a spectacularly stupid way to rethink the car, but it's pretty much how we've gone about most change in the world.

Our role is to forget everything that went before us – not to apply technology to existing solutions, but to rethink how we'd create businesses today in this context of the post-digital age.

Build data literacy fast

The promise of the post-digital age is even more data that we can access faster, process more quickly and learn more from; this is exciting but we need to be careful. The amount of data we now access has grown far faster than the general level of data literacy in companies. Most companies have too much data, it's stored in too many places, it's not 'clean' and it's often more confusing than helpful when it comes to what matters – making decisions with it. We need to ensure companies create centralized yet customer-centric data strategies, to find a way to ensure data is accessible to all in a company, useful and ultra secure.

Yet we also need to focus on using data correctly. The balance has recently swung away from decisions made on feelings, to decisions made with data. This is of concern as data is never objective; it reflects the agenda of those who collected it, filtered it and presented it. Data often presents what is most easy to measure, not what matters most, and then companies tend to optimize against aspects they can change most quickly and see happening fastest, not the things that really count.

More than anything data doesn't reflect the nuance and richness of the world. Placed in a spreadsheet, the abject horror of Penn Station in New York and the sublime beauty of Grand Central Terminal are removed. Both as measured by Excel are massive railway stations, in Manhattan, covering several city blocks, with subway and commuter lines. They are similar in every single way, yet feel different. Be careful of assessment by numbers in a world where meaning lives outside such parameters.

Reference

Levie, A (2014) The first Internet era: digitizing interfaces that already existed (catalogues newspapers). Now: creating the ones that should have existed, 14 July, available from: Twitter.com [last accessed 7 December 2017]

04
Unleashing the power of the paradigm shift

The best swordsman in the world doesn't need to fear the second-best swordsman in the world; no, the person for him to be afraid of is some ignorant antagonist who has never had a sword in his hand before; he doesn't do the thing he ought to do, and so the expert isn't prepared for him.
MARK TWAIN, 1889

It's fascinating that a quote that best explains the spirit of disruption doesn't come from a start-up founder at last year's TechCrunch or from a venture capital expert in Silicon Valley, but from a writer, more than 120 years ago, about medieval conflict. It sometimes seems that leading businesses are ignorant and antagonistic.

When the iPhone launched in 2007, it was both the best phone the world had ever seen, and Apple's first-ever phone. Dyson's first-ever vacuum cleaner was the best vacuum ever made at launch. When Tony Faddell made Nest Lab's first thermostat, it was clearly the world's best.

From Tesla's first-ever car setting the standard for the entire car industry, to Uber's first taxi business, to Amazon's first attempt at retail, it seems that the real step changes in how things are done come from those who've never done it before. Facebook is by far the biggest, most profitable media owner the world has ever seen, led by a CEO who never worked a day in his life in a media company. Donald Trump's first-ever role in politics is being the leader of the free world: he broke all the rules, he didn't let knowing nothing whatsoever about government or politics or how politicians were supposed to behave get in the way. Far from it: it raises a great question. Have these companies or people succeeded changing the game *despite* a lack of experience, or *because* of it?

Why is Space X doing things that are way beyond what NASA with its long history could do? Why did Sonos make connected speakers before Sony or Bose? Why didn't a train company invent the Hyperloop, why didn't a helicopter company invent the first drone that can carry a person, why didn't a bank or a mobile operator who owns the financial relationship with customers invent Apple Pay? Why did it take Amazon to invent the Echo speaker when Apple had Siri years earlier? The fastest growing 'TV' show today is *HQ Trivia*; it's not made by a TV company and it's not on TV, things change.

It's easy to think this is survivorship bias, that only the winners get to write history, that luck played a vital role. So in this chapter we're going to look at how this has happened. What have these companies done that is so remarkable? Why is expertise seemingly unhelpful? What does disruption mean? Most usefully of all, what can my company do about it today?

A new theory for disruption

When we talk of disruption these days, we naturally think back to Clayton Christensen's globally renowned idea that disruption is about companies who undermine legacy players based on a new technology at a lower price point.

It's based on the idea that companies are disrupted because of their success, that they are so invested in a wonderfully profitable way to extract the most money from product, and doing it so well, that they never seek to explore ways to do things differently. It is because of this happy complacency that they become vulnerable.

Then another company, using a new form of technology, enters what appears to be a different market, at a much lower price point. The new entrant suddenly or slowly expands in quality or role, to undermine the incumbent's success.

We can see how, for example, *Encyclopædia Britannica*'s expensive, yet wonderful leather books, were rapidly undermined by Wikipedia's web-based and communally resourced product. We can see how Kodak made a bucket-load of cash in the making of film and its processing, and that while they recognized the significance of digital photography, it wasn't a can of worms they wanted to open.

Now the spirit of this idea – another company with different expertise and a different way of looking at things – is a key concept, but the idea that the disruption happens from below is massively misleading. I think the idea that disruptors offer initially inferior but cheaper products is absolutely wrong.

Uber was never a cheaper way to hail a taxi; it was originally a more convenient way to get a far nicer, more expensive method of transport. Tesla's cars are by no means cheaper to buy or make, but they are changing the entire automotive industry because they have altered everything from how cars are designed and made, to how they are sold and repaired. They are slowly changing the entire automotive industry, not by being cheaper or undermining incumbents in a few ways, but by re-imagining every element in the sector.

While Airbnb may be altering many aspects of the hotel industry, and being 'disruptive', the product is vastly different; it's for people who want to stay somewhere bigger, more personal, who want to have a genuine experience. In many cases people spend more money on their stay in an Airbnb than on a hotel.

From Netflix to Facebook to Amazon to Alibaba and most of the world in which we live, the new companies that have developed have largely not been cheaper, but better. They have created better customer experiences, offered faster delivery, allowed people to do more, helped people get what they wanted. Clayton Christensen's theory does not explain how Nest became a $3.2 billion company making a far more expensive thermostat, or how Dyson was able to charge more than three times the average selling price of vacuums in 2002 and still capture a huge part of the market.

His theory does not explain how Zipcar ate into car rental markets, or how Virgin America (or Virgin Atlantic) or RedBull or Slack or WhatsApp thrive. Disruption theory does not explain the ascent of Skype, Snapchat or Buzzfeed, DJI drones or WeWork, Vice Media, BlueApron or ZocDocs, Stripe or many other modern phenomena.

It appears that 'disruption' was a theory based on selected data from a narrow window of time, on a linear world of manufacturing physical products, with examples from the world of data storage technology and excavator design around 40 years ago.

It's damaging to think of technology in that way. To base business thinking on Clayton Christensen's theory limits companies' desire and ability to see and drive more exciting opportunities. It is far more empowering, exciting, and profitable to focus on what technology can now allow us to make or what consumers really dream of having.

It is much better to focus on doing extra and more, than to be paranoid about companies undercutting you and being cheaper. We need the spirit of disruption to be about optimism and creation, not paranoia and defence.

Disruption is a rampantly overused word. It's become filler for press releases, standard issue wording for insane videos about the future and base material for PowerPoint slides. Yet, while I think Clayton Christensen's definition is no longer useful for the modern world, I do miss the fact that it was a term that meant something.

The power of the paradigm shift

How can Tesla, with less than 10 years' experience in the car industry, make vehicles that accelerate faster than any other road car ever known? Who on earth is Elon Musk to come into this category and do what is widely thought to be impossible? It takes cheek to compete with vast global car companies who employ the best electrical engineers to reinforce those companies' opinions that what Tesla is now doing isn't possible. How can the Tesla Model S P100D beat cars that are typically more than 10 times the price, with half the capacity, and despite all their competitors having 10 times more experience making cars? How can they make a car that gets better as it ages, improving overnight thanks to software updates? The Tesla Model S looks radically different to cars that are far slower, it carries five adults, it's not low to the ground. This is a car that breaks virtually all the category rules that have been formed and learned for decades. This chapter explores a totally new way to think about progress and business disruption and creates a new theory for it.

It was Thomas Kuhn, the US physicist, historian and philosopher of science, who wrote a book in 1962 called *The Structure of Scientific Revolutions* and in it coined the term 'paradigm shift' (Kuhn, 1962).

Kuhn's book focuses on the way that scientific knowledge progresses. It discusses the idea that the world comes together and gets aligned in one particular way of seeing the world that becomes fixed. Typically, there is a system of beliefs or viewpoints or universal truths which enable people to make sense of the world. At any one time, these beliefs are based on assumptions that the majority of people are happy to regard as being fixed.

This viewpoint and mental framework form the basis of other experiments and procedures, and ideally these will continue to build confidence in this viewpoint or paradigm. We are generally sure today that atoms exist, that the earth is not flat and rotates around the sun.

Yet sometimes, a breakthrough is made that challenges everything we previously thought. At this point it's clear that everything we think was known, every characteristic or variable we fixed, may no longer be the case. It's this huge shift from one way of seeing things to another that has been coined the 'paradigm shift'.

In the area of cosmology, for example, we had the notion of the earth being at the centre, a Ptolemaic viewpoint of egocentricity that was universally accepted until Copernicus proved that the sun was at the centre of the solar system, aka heliocentrism.

Poor Ptolemy is often used as an example of poor quality science and the dangers of thinking irrationally. This just isn't fair. Based on sensible assumptions and access to equipment he had available – no telescopes, limited mathematics and few people with the same level of knowledge as him – there was little wrong with his theory or methods. This is the danger of a paradigm: we seek to make sense of it more than we seek to destroy it. Humanity finds comfort in simplifying, we enjoy being right and everything making sense. It's uncomfortable to accept we may be wrong or there could be a better way. Often in life it's better to be wrong, but have everyone else be wrong too, than it is to strive for better and to be alone in being right. This is a feeling most companies can relate to.

Kuhn's theory of paradigms is generally only ever applied to scientific beliefs, or ways of seeing the world, but there is merit in the idea of tensions between groups of people who, at the time, fix assumptions, before someone smashes them and huge progress is made. I want to apply this type of mechanic to how creativity and design progress. I want to explain how disruption in business is the leap to a new paradigm, much like Kuhn's theory.

Design as evolutionary funnels

If you ask a person to draw anything on any medium with any implement, they freeze. If you ask a graphic designer to design a logo and give them nothing to work on, they can't do anything. An architect with no brief or budget, a creative in an ad agency with no problem to solve, it's all the same. Design needs constraints. All design must be shaped by elements.

Yet if you ask a group of people casually to draw a house, most people will draw something remarkably childlike and remarkably similar. We have inherently fixed in our heads an idea of what a house must be, how it is drawn, how big it will be on the paper, at what viewpoint it should come from. This preconceived idea of what a home should look like is based on how we think things should be done and how things have been done before.

We make many more assumptions than we realize when we design. They may be based on things we invented, things we remember from the past, groupthink or many other unnecessarily fixed criteria. This is natural. In a massively complex world we have to fight to make sense of, we can't continually challenge everything. We don't wake up in the morning unsure if we should accept that gravity exists, or that up isn't down; it would be exhausting. Nor can you be open to everything. If you're designing a new sofa, you can't be an expert in leather tanning and ergonomics, and then also ponder over the implications for your design of new developments in graphene (an incredibly flexible substance 200 times stronger than steel, which is currently impossible to use).

As a result, any design process follows an iterative process based on a certain set of assumptions. Normally we start with a goal or problem or brief; we then start to explore options based on design criteria; and slowly over time, collectively or individually, we improve and refine the design. Often this process isn't smooth; often progress grinds to a halt, or reaches a dead end. Generally speaking, progress towards ever better solutions starts fast, with huge initial improvements. Slowly, the process then hits what we commonly refer to as the law of diminishing returns, whereby improvements produce relatively smaller increases in output.

A key part of this process is that, as the technology matures, it tends to converge on relatively similar optimum solutions, as illustrated in Figure 4.1. Websites today look more similar to each other than when people first started designing them; hotel rooms today now look broadly alike because lessons have been shared; mobile phones once looked radically different, now they look the same. Design is like evolution – we slowly mutate and adapt in different ways, before we generally become more similar. If cosmetic surgery continues like it does today, just imagine how many people will have the 'perfect nose' in the future. Eventually, just as everything has converted to one optimal solution that everybody adopts, a paradigm leap can be made whereby the assumed parameters can change to new parameters, and a new quest towards the new optimal solution can begin, as illustrated in Figure 4.2.

Figure 4.1   A brief to the optimal solution

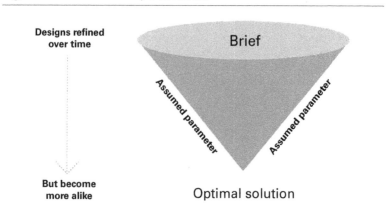

Figure 4.2   A brief to the new optimal solution

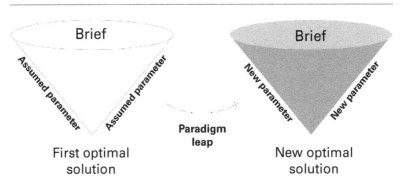

What these companies do is unleash the power of the paradigm shift. They leap from one world of possibilities to another, from one paradigm to another, to an optimal solution based on a whole new world of thinking. This is a paradigm leap, and it's the essence of disruption.

Avoiding the local maximum

Imagine, if you will, that you are walking in rather gently sloping but hilly terrain and it's very misty. For some elaborate reason you've been told to find the highest hill you can. You are likely to look around, see what looks like the most elevated terrain and walk up to it. At any moment in time your goal is to keep getting higher. If it was to get dark, your only navigational aid would be to feel that you were going uphill. It would be a sure-fire way to get to the top of that mound. Yet you will never know if that was the highest ground in the entire area, or just the only one that you could see.

This is called the difference between the local maximum and the global maximum and it's a big problem in design. In life we are unable to see all options. We don't know what material science will make possible, what new thinking will develop, or how the world will change. We can only ever go up based on what we can see. This process is illustrated in Figure 4.3, which shows the difference between the locally optimized design and the global maximum or optimal design, and the leap between them.

Figure 4.3   The leap between the locally optimized and the optimal design

The optimal design

The locally optimized design

Historically we have assumed that TV signals are best delivered by electromagnetic waves. We have assumed that near field communication (NFC) cards are the best way to make ticketing solutions for underground systems. We've long assumed that combustion engine cars are the way forward, or that magnetic resonance imaging (MRI) is the best form of scanning the body. We assume that nuclear fusion will one day be the best way to derive energy, or maglev trains will be the best way to move around. But we don't yet know for sure.

It could be that there are better solutions; it could be that when we get to the top of these peaks, we realize we should have explored another route, ascended a totally different mound. It's this process of people reaching the top of other peaks that best explains the dynamic of disruption today. Disruptive companies are those that took a different route. They saw things differently, they came to the problem from a different angle. It wasn't aeronautics experts or balloonists who pioneered powered human flight, but bicycle engineers. It's not helicopter makers who are pioneering human-carrying drones, but Chinese toy companies. We need to explore this dynamic further and investigate the actions needed.

The paradigm leap in action

On 1 July 1979, the first Sony Walkman went on sale, launching a new era in music (Haire, 2009). Sony had just created the first-ever personal music player. We could now take the music we loved with us, and without the arm-ache of the ghetto-blaster. It came at a cost. The first personal cassette players were massive, cost the equivalent of $500 at today's currency exchange rates, had terrible sound quality, skipped badly, offered awful battery life, and best (or worst!) of all, didn't even have a rewind function. We had to spin tapes around on pencils. It's wonderful to look back at our consumption of albums on tape and the thinking we did. The product was a reasonable success, selling out 30,000 units in the first three months in Japan (Adner, 2012).

Over a period of decades, with huge R&D investments from Sony and competitors alike, many errors, as well as endless rounds of customer feedback, things got much, much better. Not least the name. First marketed in the USA as the Soundabout, it was soon changed to the Walkman, and came in a choice of colours. Despite the competition, Sony kept ahead of its rivals. Even 10 years after its first device, Sony's Walkman retained a 50 per cent market share in the USA and 46 per cent in Japan, in a space seething with competitors. Sony maintained its profit margin, regardless of the entry of many new competitors to the market, with a price premium of approximately $20 over rival offers (Adner, 2012).

Over time the device improved. It got Dolby (B, then C), rechargeable batteries, even rewind buttons. Engineers got better at making components smaller, as they always do, so the size of the personal cassette player got smaller, until finally, with a smart aluminium casing, it was only a little bigger than the cassette itself. Miniaturization wasn't easy, batteries needed to be improved, motors needed to get more efficient, step-up converters were invented and made smaller. At the same time the device got *way* cheaper. By 2002 it wasn't uncommon to see personal radio cassette players in gas stations for those impulse purchases on the go. Designers had fun: we got sports models with yellow plastic, radio functions were added. Life was good.

The improvements came fast then slowed down, and it got to a point where the improvements got smaller. It was easy to reduce the size initially but once it had shrunk to barely bigger than a cassette tape, improvements were marginal, and the law of diminished returns we mentioned earlier set in.

The Walkman is what changed our relationship with music. It became something we could curate, copy, and take with us. It made us love music, and as a soundtrack to our life, it was the background music that embellished what we had.

The CD player era

At the time the Walkman design peaked – the very best music-playing machine the world had ever collectively crafted – came the very worst personal CD player ever made. It was huge, far more expensive than the best Walkman it replaced at $450, and had an awful battery life. It would skip all the time. The LCD display was tiny and displayed very little information. It was the worst CD player ever, but it was still better than the best Walkman. This was digital sound. It came with no tape degradation and no winding in the spaghetti after an accident.

We'd made a paradigm leap. We'd gone from ever smaller, incremental design improvements that worked towards an increasingly easy-to-envision optimal goal, with everyone on the same page and working towards solving the same problems, to a whole new canvas for design where the end result wasn't clear.

We now had new criteria against which to optimize design, new constraints to shape the progress towards the optimal design and new problems to solve. The criteria that once held back the cassette player were different. The problems to solve now were new and the expertise needed wildly different. Laser engineers replaced electromagnetic sensor experts and Dolby engineers were replaced by people who knew about caching digital memory to stop skipping. Designers who loved slow, high-torque motors now needed to know about fast-spinning, low-torque designs.

Even recording music faced new challenges. How do you compress music without making it seem cold and flat? Can you remove information about frequencies we can't hear, without changing the soul of the music? Even breaking up music from continuous to segmented had rather profound meanings: for example, is it okay to have 'tracks' of a few seconds between other tracks or should those little warm-up flurries or contextual introductions be attached to the song?

The worst MP3 players

As Discmans became marvellously cheap, remarkably thin, and music moved from analogue to digital, someone had a new idea: what if the physical media wasn't needed? What if the music was lifted and liberated from the storage medium and was stored in the music player? This was a huge shift. Until now music had been physical, and media had been too. We lived with VHS tapes, magazines, CDs, laser disks. Media was something we bought and touched. Facing high costs of storage, music could only be digitized if it was compressed and the MP3 format was born.

The first-ever MP3 player was of course both marvellous and awful. It was launched in 1997 by Saehan Information Systems, and sold as its 'MPMan' player in Asia in spring 1998 (Van Buskirk, 2005). While the battery power was fine, the device small and not too expensive, new issues arose. User experience was a concern. To put music into the device, the music first had to be encoded in the MP3 format by an encoder provided by the user, and then transferred via the parallel port to the docking station that connected to the portable player device. Another issue was storage: the two versions of the player offered 32 or 64MBs of capacity, enough to store a measly 6 or 12 songs, less than most albums.

There were legal issues too. MP3 files were not readily available. The Recording Industry Association of America (RIAA) Associate Director of Anti-Copyright Infringement, Frank Creighton, initially said the MPMan had 'no function other than playing material that was stolen from record companies' (Kaufman, 1998).

It's here we first see the uncomfortable relationship between regulation and the law and the spirit of disruption, a topic we will visit later in this book.

The problems the MP3 player brought with it were again totally new. The company that would produce a breakthrough wouldn't be Sony, with their amazing engineers who'd perfected CDs and lasers and cassettes and motors. It wouldn't be a company that knew batteries better than anyone. It wouldn't be material scientists who could make things thinner. It would be people who understood the human-centred design experience. People who knew that in this era, how the product functioned was not the most vital thing. It would be companies that understood software and who were also large enough to negotiate with the record industry and be taken seriously. It was of course unlikely to be a company like Sony, who were making too much money selling physical music.

What made the iPod successful wasn't the iPod. It was iTunes, and it took time. Steve Jobs knew that on its own the MP3 player was useless. He knew that in order for the device to have value, other building blocks needed to be in place first. The success of the iPod would be dependent not on a better device, but on a better ecosystem: a faster internet to make downloading songs fast enough, record labels to be ready to sell music as MP3 files. He realized that innovation was never about being first per se, but to be first in a meaningful way *at the right time*.

The first-generation iPod for Mac retailed at $399 and could store up to 1,000 songs. It was a revelation. Now you could take any piece of music you could ever hope to own with you. It had an intuitive interface design and was lightweight. Despite being available only for Mac users, which was 10 per cent of all computer users at the time, the iPod was the fastest selling MP3 player to ever hit the market (Adner, 2012).

We had entered the paradigm where software mattered more than hardware. Apple announced the iTunes Music Store, an online retail hub to browse and purchase music for 99 cents per song and within two years iTunes' library had grown to 1.5 million songs. Apple had understood the relationship between service and device. It would make little profit from selling songs at 99 cents per download, but the ecosystem mattered. The iTunes store gave the iPod legitimacy in a world of shady MP3 accessibility.

MP3 players got better, but not quite in the same way. They got smaller and lighter, storage was increased, devices were cheaper, but progress felt different. It was more about the interface. Apple iTunes was most people's main experience of the device. It became about how easy it was to find music, how nice it felt to do so. It became about reducing the pain points of coding music in such a way that it aided distribution, or digital rights management protection. It was about making payment easy, making synchronizing seem obvious. More than anything else, Apple had to guide people into a new way of thinking about music in the easiest way possible. Again, the skills needed were different and put the focus on coders, not engineers, as well as user interface design, not product design. Deals had to be made with record labels rather than with aluminium rollers. Most core Apple staff skills were more useful in this paradigm.

Our relationship with technology changed too. We expected to own more, to listen to what we wanted when we wanted. We'd skip things we didn't love or feel like at that time. Technology started to shape how we behaved now, not reflect how we behaved then.

iPods took over the world, music became digital and the development of the internet and the shift to the smartphone brought another huge paradigm shift.

The streaming age

The internet meant we no longer needed to own music, we just needed access to it. As home broadband became more prevalent and 3G connectivity spread on phones, we no longer needed to store music or to own music; we just needed to access it, at all times, immediately.

And this is where we are now. The world of portable music blends into the world of smartphone design. We now find ourselves with faster connectivity, better battery life, a need for music videos, for higher resolution screens, for larger OLED screens. The whole paradigm has shifted again.

Phones have changed so much of our lives and so many industries. Even in the specific context of music, they changed more than we ever realized, and they once again changed our relationship with music. Walkmans allowed us to take music with us, to augment our lives; CDs allowed us to listen only to the music we loved, we could skip tracks immediately; MP3 players allowed us to think of music with abundance not scarcity; and streaming meant we discovered and selected music in new ways.

Streaming means the new challenges are of managing abundance, aiding discovery, and making money in this era. Our relationship moved from the album to the single, from the record label to the content gateway. The distribution costs of music, the hosting and the production, tended to zero.

We no longer needed record labels to make well-produced music and distribute it. We no longer needed companies to merchandise it, nor albums bundled as units to 'buy' and to access music. We had a relationship with the band or artist and the stuff we loved. We became directly connected to what we wanted. We are now firmly in the streaming age. We care about Spotify or Apple Music or Pandora, we don't care about physical media, record labels, bitrates, and costs.

Leaps in design paradigms surround us

The changes in music device follow a set pattern: technology and design make radical progress, which then slows to find an optimal device, followed by a huge leap to another way of thinking. This is not something unique to personal music. We see these leaps everywhere.

When transporting goods in the UK for example, for millennia we functioned with the paradigm of transporting goods by horse, before a sudden move to shipping goods by canal resulted in increased construction of canals. These canals improved in their set-up and construction over time, to be replaced dramatically by the advent of a cheaper and faster method of transporting goods: railway. Railway technology in turn progressed in huge leaps and bounds before being destroyed again by the use of large trucks transporting goods via roads.

With personal transportation we've had the era of horseback riding, then horse-drawn cars, then combustion-powered horseless carriages, and now it looks as if we're on the edge of the next paradigm, electric-powered cars. It appears the entire infrastructure of petrol stations will soon need to be rebuilt for electric cars. In the near future we may go from the era of owning cars to the era of getting access to self-driving cars. We are unlikely to own them, but we may rent access much like a data plan on a mobile phone. Suddenly car parking spaces are entirely freed up as cars can move around freely and out of cities when demand is lower. Suddenly our commutes may become longer and more productive and the shape and size of cities may change. Cars themselves will change. Vehicles are currently designed to be suitable for all the most common types of usage. A typical adult needs a car that fits five people, can travel at 85mph and can do 400-mile journeys with ease, even if they drive it alone 95 per cent of the time, at less than 40 mph and do fewer than 40 miles per day. If we are to access self-driving cars there is no reason why they shouldn't be much more specialized vehicles. We may have lounge-like vehicles stacked with large screens and room for eight people for multi-family trips. We may see absurd luxury cars that fit two people for couples' romantic week-ends, or pod-like vehicles that fit one person and no luggage, travel at less than 50 mph and act only for commuters. More will change in this paradigm than anyone realizes.

We have had eras of shopping: the local store, the department store, the shopping mall and now online stores. Paradigms are everywhere. We once kept time with sundials, then had large mechanical clocks in town centres, then mechanical pocket watches, quartz watches and now two-thirds of teenagers don't carry a watch at all, they use their phone (Clark, 2007). It's likely one day we'll have health sensors or payment bands on our wrists instead.

The phone has eaten other devices too. We had the paradigm of the *camera obscura*, then the photographic camera, the digital camera, and now we just tend to use phones. Initially, smartphones increased demand for proper cameras, before becoming so good that they ate that market. We had black & white cathode ray tubes in televisions once, then the colour CRT TV, then we saw plasma TVs develop, to be overtaken by LCD and then LED TVs. Yet now increasingly we watch videos on our phones and not on the television.

The world of currency and money has had similar shifts: we had the era of cowrie shells and other forms of items of rareness, then we shifted and coins developed, and we had units of money with an intrinsic value. We then leapt to the idea of banknotes, the concept of the promissory note where something had no inherent value but was deemed by all to be trusted. We then shifted to another paradigm with the first credit cards, where the entire transaction was unattached to the physical token (a credit card isn't a note, it's a shortcut to a digital transaction). Now we tend to use physical currency less and less, we use formal bank and credit card transactions less, we use apps like Venmo or WeChat Pay or Alipay. In China today, $5 trillion of payments each year are done this way (Cheng, 2017). It's likely that the bank of the future will soon largely operate with digital wallets, not physical locations.

And before we get comfortable with that, we could be about to see an even newer era of money: cryptocurrencies in which, rather than systems controlled by central banks and centralized control systems, money is digitalized, based on artificial scarcity and control by distributed communities of people.

Paradigms are complex

It's been ages since I've paid with cowrie shells, but right now I do have coins, banknotes, credit cards, and money in a digital wallet. I nearly bought Bitcoins in 2011, but alas I got scared. In the same way that we may own Walkmans and Discmans and an iPod, paradigms typically overlap. Even in the UK canal use is coming back, as are vinyl records, but it's normally obvious which is the paradigm of the future. I would not want to bet my company on the success of quartz watches, railways, shopping malls or the combustion engine.

Sometimes the future arrives and then vanishes too. In 1900, electric cars were so popular that in New York City there was a fleet of electric taxis, and electric cars made up a third of all vehicles on the road. But Henry Ford's ability to make the petrol-driven Model T for less than half the price soon put an end to electric cars (Strohl, 2010). Direct shopping that avoided physical retail isn't new either. One of the first mail-order catalogues, was selling scientific and academic books (just as Amazon started), and was set up by Benjamin Franklin in 1744 (Woloson, 2013). Mail order has long preceded e-commerce, yet strangely the businesses like Sears, Freemans, Montgomery Ward or SkyMall, that seemed to have the perfect structural foundation to win in the age of e-commerce, all survived until the internet took off and have since generally performed badly. Certainly none has gone close to accomplishing what Amazon has done. The lesson here is that it is only in retrospect that we can see what will win and sometimes you can be constructed perfectly for the future, and still mess it up.

The lesson from the paradigm shift: we have to break rules

Disruption is the art of identifying which parts of the past are no longer relevant to the future, and exploiting that delta at all costs.
LEVIE, 2014

We need to be clear that these shifts are always enormous. Within one specific industry, huge changes happen. The most successful companies the world has ever seen are typically those to enter a new paradigm with the first reasonable product. There is another theory from Jean-Marie Dru, the chairman of Global Advertising Agency TBWA, that he set out in 1996, around the same time as Clayton Christensen proposed his theory of disruption. Jean-Marie Dru's theory was that disruption was about establishing category norms, finding the ways that everyone solved problems, and then specifically and precisely ignoring one of those rules.

My new theory for disruption is based on the idea that companies don't go against category norms; they just base their approach on brand new thinking and change the parameters that fixed the design process.

Don't let expertise or success kill you

At every stage, the new era demands totally new assumptions, different thinking, and a step change in performance. Often the dominant player changes, the incumbents build on the expertise of the past whereas the insurgent isn't bogged down by expertise. What in theory should allow dominant players to win easily often acts against them. It's not just that having a large network of banks on the high street, huge access to capital, a great reputation and trust with consumers isn't that helpful if the world switches to cryptocurrencies or digital wallets; it's that you are so invested in the old paradigm, that you actively seek to combat change. Sony made too much money from selling music. Kodak made too much money selling photography products.

Being different is scary

In the early days of Amazon Jeff Bezos needed over 60 meetings to raise $1 million. He was laughed out of many rooms, with most people first asking him, 'What's the internet?' Being different is hard (Sawers, 2012). Even as recently as 2013, Matthew Yglesias called it a 'charitable institution being run by elements of the investment community for the benefit of consumers' (Yglesias, 2013). A lot of people don't like businesses that appear to break rules.

When Roger Bannister broke the four-minute mile, he risked what doctors agreed would probably kill any man. Rules and assumptions are there to make us feel better, but they also hold us back.

Don't apply old thinking to new eras

In 1994 the UK catalogue company Freemans saw the future and it was digital. It didn't create a website to buy from, it didn't do customer service and accept orders via e-mail. No, they took the entire catalogue, scanned it into images and distributed it on a CD. Often, we get thinking wrong. Coin was a well-funded start-up whose whole inception was based on the fact that affluent customers had many credit cards, and thus created a 'digital' credit card, which for a mere $100 would store many credit cards digitally. You could then select which card you wanted to pay for with a few taps and pay that way. Few realized at the time that Apple Pay was about to launch. Redbox spent millions solving the problems of Blockbuster DVD rental by placing thousands of DVD rental machines around the nation. Just as video streaming was taking off. We have to build for the right paradigm.

When people see VR headsets and want to create shopping malls within them, you realize the degree to which imagination fails us. We have to work around new parameters and new behaviours, not lazily transpose our thinking into the new one.

Don't apply old models to new eras

We tend to need data in modern business. We need to see ROI projections of things that don't exist yet. Yet those are success criteria from an out-of-touch era. When I grew up, even in safe rural England, there were three rules that were clearer than any others. One, never get in a stranger's car. Two, never go to a stranger's house. And three, ideally and if possible, don't even talk to strangers. Yet we now live in a world where Uber, Airbnb and Tinder have built some of the world's most successful businesses off the back of contradicting the rules we have all grown up with.

Amazon is showing the light at the end of the tunnel. After years of burning money in its retail offering, subsidized by the profits of its web services division, you can now see that it could finally get big enough to make money. As it becomes so large it kills others in the space, as it becomes so big it can put even more pressure on the incumbents in the space, as it decides to launch its own-label goods, we can see how a model that worked okay in the previous paradigm could actually lead to rampant success in the next.

Uber is the same. Uber can't ever justify its valuation today as a 'taxi killer'. The world's taxi market isn't enough to justify anything close to its valuation. But if Uber can become so big, so fast and, above all else, work in rural areas effectively, it's no longer competing with taxi ridership, but all forms of personal mobility. When we can get a train to a large town and hail an Uber, when we can commute to work in rural areas with an Uber, all of a sudden, the model and the valuation *can* make sense.

Ignore most future models

The skill to thinking about the future isn't to look at precise trend lines from the past and linearly project them forward, it's not to obsess over technology, it's to be empathetic to people, it's to consider thoughtfully what enhances human feelings, what addresses our concerns, it's to layer through use cases and to feel our way ahead. I don't think large spreadsheet-oriented companies are best placed to do this.

Data is not always helpful. People are poor forecasters of their own future intent. We all love to make sense of complexity with a model; the Gartner Hype Cycle is a lovely way to confidently track technologies as they rise and fall, but it's not actually proven to be useful. It has failed to track the actual path of most technologies.

References

Adner, R (2012) *The Wide Lens: A new strategy for innovation,* Portfolio Penguin, New York City

Cheng, E (2017) Cash is already pretty much dead in China as the country lives the future with mobile pay, *CNBC,* 08 October, available from:

https://www.cnbc.com/2017/10/08/china-is-living-the-future-of-mobile-pay-right-now.html [last accessed 7 December 2017]

Clark, A (2007) Wear a watch? What for? *CBS News*, 16 February, available from: https://www.cbsnews.com/news/wear-a-watch-what-for/ [last accessed 7 December 2017]

Haire, M (2009) A brief history of the Walkman, *Time*, 1 July, available from: http://content.time.com/time/nation/article/0,8599,1907884,00.html [last accessed 7 December 2017]

Kaufman, G (1998) MPMAN threatens conventional record business, MTV, 4 May, available from: http://www.mtv.com/news/150202/mpman-threatens-conventional-record-business/ [last accessed 7 December 2017]

Kuhn, T (1962) *The Structure of Scientific Revolutions,* University of Chicago Press, Chicago

Levie, A (2014) Disruption is the art of identifying which parts of the past are no longer relevant to the future, and exploiting that delta at all costs [Twitter] 13 April, available from: Twitter.com [last accessed 7 December 2017]

Sawers, P (2012) Jeff Bezos attended 60 investor meetings to raise $1m from 22 people, just to get Amazon started, *The Next Web*, 29 November, available from: https://thenextweb.com/media/2012/11/29/in-the-early-days-amazon-founder-jeff-bezos-attended-60-investor-meetings-to-raise-1m-from-22-people/ [last accessed 7 December 2017]

Strohl, D (2010) Henry Ford and the electric car, *Hemmings Daily*, 25 May, available from: https://www.hemmings.com/blog/index.php/2010/05/25/henry-ford-and-the-electric-car/ [last accessed 7 December 2017]

Twain, M (1889) *A Connecticut Yankee in King Arthur's Court*, Charles L Webster and Co., New York City

Van Buskirk, E (2005) Bragging rights to the world's first MP3 player, *CNet*, 25 January, available from: https://www.cnet.com/uk/news/bragging-rights-to-the-worlds-first-MP3-player/ [last accessed 7 December 2017]

Woloson, W (2013) How Benjamin Franklin invented the mail-order business, *Bloomberg View*, 13 March, available from: https://www.bloomberg.com/view/articles/2013-03-13/how-benjamin-franklin-invented-the-mail-order-business [last accessed 7 December 2017]

Yglesias, M (2013) Jeff Bezos explains Amazon's strategy for world domination, *Slate*, 12 April, available from: http://www.slate.com/blogs/moneybox/2013/04/12/amazon_as_corporate_charity_jeff_bezos_says_there_s_a_method_to_the_madness.html [last accessed 7 December 2017]

PART TWO
Unleashing the power of now

05
Digital transformation

In my experience, the two biggest questions an innovation endeavour must first ask are rarely raised. The first is why are you doing it, and the second is how much are you really prepared to change? We need to ask whether we are prepared to make changes right down at the core of the business, at the very foundations on which it is built.

We need to stop thinking of technology as a tattoo, a surface-level commitment best kept on a conspicuous but infrequently used part of the body. Instead, let's think of it as oxygen: essential to the beating heart of your business. In this chapter, we will explore the idea of the depth to which we apply new thinking and technology. We need to raise the issue of, and tightly define, digital transformation. It's only by starting to see what a powerful lever technology is that we can see the size of the gains possible for businesses that get transformation right.

An era of bolted-on change

Remember the millennium (Y2K) bug? Potentially, it was the moment when we'd realize the whole world's software was created on a foundation that wasn't built to handle it. The virtual world would come crumbling down, planes would drop out of the sky… and it never happened.

So we kept building.

When airlines now routinely face software crashes that ground their entire fleet of planes, it seems odd that companies with such good apps, with iPads for pilots, flying the most advanced aircraft in the world, could suffer from such a fundamental flaw. When week after week we see large retailers hacked and their data stolen, it seems remarkable that they can offer such incredible logistical marvels to keep products on shelves, yet be so open and vulnerable to destruction. A glitch in the New York Stock Exchange causes a shutdown with increasing frequency, and yet this seems at odds with a world of trillions of dollars flowing at the speed of light with the fastest processing the world has ever seen.

I'd proffer the thought that this is all too common, that companies built for the past may offer glimpses into the incredible, but are mired in vulnerabilities in other places. Modern-day businesses are asymmetric constructs: a legacy of patches, quick fixes, hacks, workarounds, and hope.

If IT systems and processes were visualized as engineering, and companies as buildings, we'd see unwieldy buildings, the ugliest, messiest structures we've ever known. Oddly shaped towers, temporary structures and hatchet jobs, built on non-existent foundations, mixtures of prevailing engineering theorems that got fashioned together with steel and concrete wherever possible. Our buildings would be the messiest, heaviest, clumsiest buildings ever known. They would work pretty much all the time, but we'd worry about the days when too many people visited, or the wind was strong, when they would just about work out, but not be what you set out for. They would be a total mess, and we'd see it.

From Slack to Shyp, from Blue Apron to WeWork, Upwork to Seamless, Postmates to Handy, I'm getting increasingly spoiled by companies that seem simply *to work*. How is it that the online news site Quartz can both make a book and create one of the nicest and best functioning retail sites I've ever seen?

A lot of it is about attitude. As we look around us, the world is a monument to companies that have never really wanted to embrace the digital age. At each and every turn, and seemingly with all business decisions, we encounter companies whose digital body language has been poor while it's been saying the right things. It's a landscape of companies that, at best, created small units to manage this change and, at worst, have entirely buried their heads in the sand. I don't understand how a brand-new luxury hotel in Peru is even able to *buy* a phone dock that doesn't work for a phone made after 2004, let alone decides it's the best purchase decision to make.

Onions

There is a theory in social science that the characteristics and attributes of people can be best represented by a stacked Euler diagram, or more easily visualized as an onion. The work in social penetration theory, started by Irwin Altman and Dalmas Taylor, suggests that people are based around concentric layers, the most superficial and visible behaviours on the edge, the innermost and existential at the heart or core.

The easiest aspect of people to see is behaviour, the outermost layer. A little deeper in the onion is our knowledge and skills. The next layer within the onion is our attitudes. These are the core ways in which we think about the world, how we tend to behave and how we understand and make sense of the world. They are our default ways of dealing with situations and are typically built upon our values – the next layer in.

Our values are deep. They develop slowly over time in response to our experiences. Values take months or years to change. Values are central to who we are as a person. They are a representation of how we interact with the world, how we make decisions, how we go about our life. But they are not the core element of who we are. At the very heart of the onion lie personality and ability. These are the very foundational elements of who we are.

I don't think anyone would agree that companies are people, but the analogy of onions works well to better understand the structure of businesses, what drives them to be what they are and what layers make them up. Figure 5.1 illustrates this concept of multi-layered companies.

Imagine your business as an onion, as a series of concentric layers around a small core, each and every layer built on top of the next innermost layer. We can start to make sense of the complex structures of businesses and how they do everything from finding meaning

Figure 5.1 The conceptual layers of a company

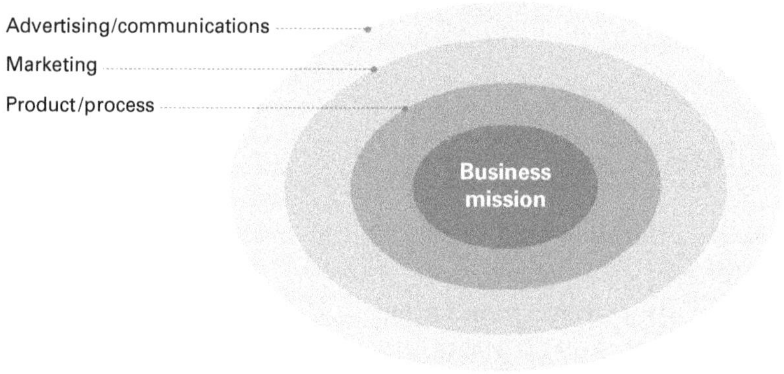

Advertising/communications
Marketing
Product/process

Business
mission

to making products, creating and supporting brands. The following section, which moves from the outermost to the innermost layers, illustrates the similarities between personality traits and business traits.

The communications layer: the outermost layer

For businesses, people's behaviour equates to the communications they put out: the paid-for, controlled messages of advertising and the websites they own, or of the brand's and the business's PR strategy These are the environments where companies proactively decide what the world or their target audience should think of them. They are the places where the company gets to control most tightly 'the message' and most precisely visualize and make real 'the brand'. This layer explains to the world what it is that a company makes. Communications can be:

- owned media like websites and stores, brochures, blogs, or e-mail newsletters;
- earned media like reviews, PR, organic search;
- paid media, which is primarily what we've always thought of as advertising – paid media placements where the business gets to control the message entirely.

The marketing layer: supporting communications

Supporting the communications layer would be the marketing layer, a much more diverse array of activities that a company undertakes to both sell products and create the brand. You could argue that it is this layer that creates the full meaning of brand and the full understanding in a consumer's mind of what a product or service is, what it means, what it's worth and more. This layer includes:

- Place: the geographical location where the product is offered, the type of distribution channel used and increasingly the strategy behind distribution – placement both in terms of where the product is for sale, as well as the context and precise location within the store or online where the product is found.

- Pricing: the amount a customer pays for a product or the sacrifice or effort people are prepared to make to acquire a product.

- Promotion: generally, the sum of all marketing communications is to make the offer or brand known and understood to potential and current customers in order to persuade them to take an interest or buy the product. This is generally understood to include advertising, PR, sales promotion, direct marketing, and increasingly, influencer marketing, owned media, sponsorship and a dazzling array of new techniques or even old techniques which for some reason are considered new again, like branded content or native advertising. It's this part of the marketing layer that the outermost communications layer most directly builds on.

The product layer: what you make

The product layer is the 'what' of a company: the part of the business that represents its reason for existence. It's effectively the mechanics of how a company operates and the product it makes, but in the broadest terms. Products are increasingly deemed to be more than just the tangible physicality of a product. Car companies are not just about the experience of having the car, but the experience of buying and maintaining the car. The business of mobile network companies is less about providing data and voice well, and more about having quality service, providing access to unique content, building partnerships with useful tangential services, and much more.

In the modern age, products encompass everything that you experience as an owner or user. They include all touchpoints: the check-in desk at the airport; the clerk at the bank; from the form you fill in to get insurance to the terms and conditions, the labelling and merchandising of the policy. Products run deep. For example, in cars they include the after-sales service, the e-mails before your lease ends, the feeling of ownership in its totality.

The process layer: the how

The process layer is the 'how' of a company: everything that gets things made. It includes the culture and how people are expected to behave, how and why people are recruited, the training they undertake, and the spirit and attitudes they are likely to have and represent. Is the company autocratic, democratic or (unlikely) holocratic? Are people empowered to make decisions or hiding in a culture of fear? Does the company seek to outsource as much as possible or keep control? Process is the organizational chart, the way decisions get made, meetings are arranged, how people are judged and supported, promoted and fired. It covers systems too, the technology used to underpin a company. Does it use Slack, Dropbox, video-conferencing software? What are the security features like, is the company open-plan or tucked away in cubicles, is it open- or closed-minded?

Mission

It's hard to understate the importance of the mission, yet few companies have one. If Nike says, 'If you have a body, you are an athlete' and that their role is to 'bring inspiration and innovation to every athlete in the world' then you know what you are supposed to be doing and not doing when you work there. If IKEA stands for 'making everyday life better for our customers with well-designed products' it's pretty empowering. The mission is the raison d'être: it's why everyone goes to work, it's how people focus, celebrate, prioritize. The mission of the company is what supports everything else. It drives and reinforces the culture and processes, which then design, refine and make the products and experiences, and which are then communicated to the market.

So we get new questions. How deeply are you applying new technology? What is the new context in which you now operate? What new consumer behaviours can you work around and leverage?

A prioritization framework for innovation

When Andy Warhol said that everyone would be famous for 15 minutes, he understood the modern era well. It sometimes seems that everyone in business is trying to build a personal brand, get a following, be retweeted or faved, or whatever your preferred terms of approval are.

As I will discuss later, we are impatient for success, we seek change that is fast, easy and tangible, more than stuff that makes a difference. If we were to draw a matrix plotting change from easy to difficult on one axis, and the amount of difference brought about by that change from irrelevant to vital on the other, we'd have a matrix like the one in Figure 5.2. We don't favour the change that makes a difference, but the one that we can do most easily.

We would expect subjective, sensible, strategic business minds to care less about what is fast, and more about what is profound. We would expect that people would first of all focus on the most transformative projects, the ones that will profoundly reduce costs, or increase revenue, or ideally both. Often the things that really make a difference are rather boring: a new distribution centre in Kansas; a new invoicing backbone; an entirely new way to process payments in a bank; rethinking your customer relationship management (CRM) strategy and data architecture to manage customers over the long term, send them personalized e-mails, and ensure you don't send new

Figure 5.2   Problems and opportunities matrix

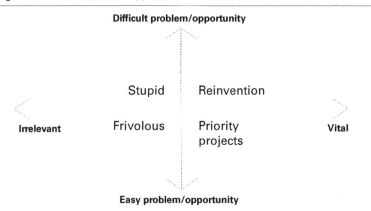

sign-up offers to existing customers. These things run deep. If a car company is really keen to get CRM right, then the dealership data needs to talk to the Tier 2 dealer network, which then needs to work with HQ data. Each of these systems has probably been built by different people, at different times on different systems. If a fast-food company is going to improve its customer service at all its locations, it's going to have to work with thousands of tiny franchise operators as well as those large franchise owners that can be a bit of a pain in the neck. A lot of the things that will actually make a difference are very hard to do, but as human nature wants us to feel as if we've achieved something, we focus on what we can do most readily and which requires least cooperation with other people.

It's pretty easy to innovate at the edge

The outermost (communications) layer offers the easiest possible innovation. It requires the least organizational effort, the most super-ficial of conversations, is easiest and fastest to achieve and is the most highly visible.

Innovation at the communications layer is also the fastest way to show the world you're ahead of the industry. Deliver a can of coke to construction workers in Jakarta with a drone and stick the video on

YouTube. Job done. Place a vending machine in a shopping mall in Dubai and give free ice creams to those who smile, make a case study video, overlay some U2 – and celebrate at Cannes. Create an app where you upload swishes of your hair to Instagram and get someone famous to tweet the winner – this is easy.

Communications innovation in the digital age just requires embracing new platforms, new gadgets, new start-ups – and away we go. Innovation at this level is normally pretty cheap, involves few stakeholders internally, can be outsourced to agencies and is quite easy to get a budget for. If you want to spend $50,000 on a chatbot, the money comes quite quickly as the PR results can usually be easily measured to show success. If you want to give an iBeacon start-up $25,000 to try something in one location or $100,000 for a VR experience at a tradeshow, then you won't need to reach far upstream into your client's complex organizational politics. In fact, you can probably get rewarded with some decent press merely for announcing an intent to do something.

Communications-level innovation is everywhere. The pages of TechCrunch and *Adweek* are littered with emoji hacks, buttons on shoes to order pizza, a 360-video ad on Facebook, something with a 3D-printed trinket, and the award winners in most advertising festivals feature heavily with this fast, snackable, digestible, quick innovation. Realistically, in my role as head of innovation in a large global media agency, it is my job to do this. I want to make my clients look good, to find new partners to work with, to do small incremental projects that push boundaries. The problem is that it rarely makes a difference to the bottom line. It's all innovation for innovation's sake, never or rarely to make a difference.

Innovation at the marketing level

Innovation at the marketing layer makes a bigger difference, but is harder to bring about. Dollar Shave Club, Warby Parker, Casper and Wayfair are examples of companies that have considered new ways to go to market, new ways to price or distribute. They have gone against many industry norms, but are not, at the core, radically different companies to their predecessors. At this layer, change is much harder. IKEA seems to find it extremely hard to create an online business when they know it is store visits that drive incremental and impulse purchases, when they know delivering furniture isn't cheap and they've got billions invested in retail footprint to serve people another way. Yet unlike many, IKEA is working hard to change, announcing partnerships with third-party companies to find ways to sell online more efficiently (Meixler, 2017).

Better examples include companies such as e.l.f. Cosmetics. The company started with only 13 make-up products, and its launch was inspired when the founders saw women with expensive cars buying bargain-price cosmetics at 99-cent stores in Los Angeles. It has a very simple, tiered pricing approach, selling high-quality cosmetics at $1, $3, and $6 price points. The company launched online only when it realized that the only way to get a listing and a feature in *Glamour* magazine was to ensure that products could be distributed nation-wide. The company shuns any paid advertising but uses influencers and social media to spread the word and hosts an active blog that includes celebrity sightings.

Applying new thinking at the process layer: the how

Going deeper into the core of the business, we now consider those companies that apply new thinking and new technology to the product and process layer.

Companies like Blue Apron have not changed everything about food or grocery retail, but they have totally transformed how we buy it. They've taken industry norms and turned them on their heads. They don't sell ready-made meals, as many before have tried. They sell pre-measured ingredients, with beautiful packaging, wonderful instructions, based on a subscription model. They lock the customer into a relationship with a company providing meals on demand, but with the added pleasure of cooking the meal yourself.

Deeper transformation: companies built with new thinking at the core

The companies that are truly different are those that have applied new thinking and new technology, and have worked around new customer behaviours and expectations at the very core of their business. They have taken tech to the very heart of what they do.

The examples are clear and notable. We can look at Amazon, Alibaba, Facebook, Google. This offers another chance to talk about Airbnb. Figure 5.3, based on data from Bloomberg, shows the ascent of the largest public companies today since the launch of the iPhone in 2007, and demonstrates how modern-thinking, software-focused companies have exploded, while banks and energy companies have fallen in value. The world's seven most valuable public companies are all in the technology sector.

However, even more interesting to investigate are those companies we don't often think about.

One such example is Lemonade, a simple contents insurance brand based in the USA. They built their entire company around app-based mobile devices, using chat-like interfaces. They even employ sophisticated AI techniques to automate most of their service. But the re-imagination goes way beyond that. Insurance companies have long been rooted in the design theory of 'dark patterns'. They make

Figure 5.3 The world's most valuable public companies, November 2017

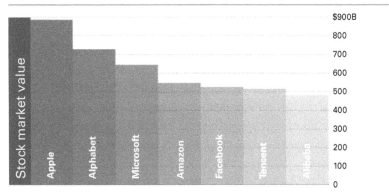

SOURCE Bloomberg

more money by denying claims and by discouraging them in the first place. Lemonade has completely turned the thinking on its head. Claims are paid near instantly, and are extremely easy to make using the chat interface. But the most remarkable feature is that you make your claim by recording a video testimony with your phone's front-facing camera. It is both quick and easy, and is also likely to weed out those people who would feel uncomfortable lying on camera.

There are other companies who remain uncelebrated but who are remarkably different. The mobile payments service Venmo, for example, does not charge for most of its transactions and allows people to send money to each other instantly. The business currently makes very little money, but could one day become a digital wallet, allowing people to buy things from shops and services, not just pay money to each other. Given the transaction fees that credit card companies charge, it's easy to see how Venmo could make money fast with a new model. Other examples include TransferWise, which is a simple way to send money internationally at much fairer rates, and LendingClub which offers peer-to-peer loans.

It seems that the speed of growth and increase in value of the world's most successful companies are both closely correlated with their use of technology and (more importantly) the depth at which they apply it in their business. Figure 5.4 illustrates how some of the world's top valued companies have grown exponentially since the release of the iPhone in 2007, thus offering a glimpse of how just one technology can unleash usability and the real potential for their services.

Digitization vs digital transformation

It's interesting to compare how deeply people really take new thinking on board. In my opinion there is a huge gulf between companies retroactively applying new technology to old processes and systems and those having the courage to dig more deeply, invest more money and make deeper changes.

Tesco started its dotcom operations way back in 1996 with the help of a fax machine. Initially they built a simple website, took some

Figure 5.4 The smartphone era: market-value rankings of companies since the first iPhone launched

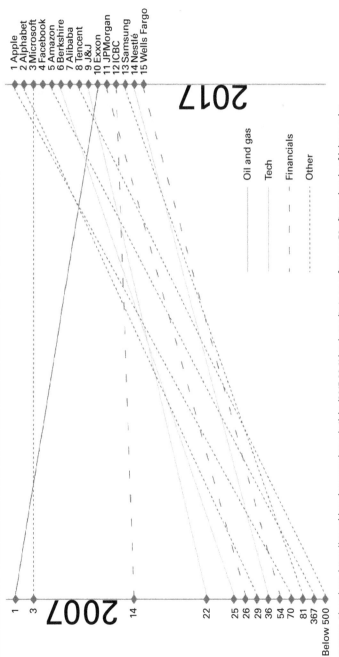

1 Apple
2 Alphabet
3 Microsoft
4 Facebook
5 Amazon
6 Berkshire
7 Alibaba
8 Tencent
9 J&J
10 Exxon
11 JPMorgan
12 ICBC
13 Samsung
14 Nestlé
15 Wells Fargo

2017

2007

1
3
14
22
25
26
29
36
54
70
81
367
Below 500

Oil and gas
Tech
Financials
Other

SOURCE Bloomberg, https://www.bloomberg.com/news/articles/2017-09-11/apple-vaults-to-no-1-from-no-70-after-a-decade-of-iphone-sales

photos of what they normally sold and put them online. Quite soon orders began to come through rapidly to stores all around the UK. Realizing what they'd done, they quickly established a new procedure. Those orders for 'online' received at head office were faxed out to individual branches, where the overnight stock replenishers would pick the items ordered. This is the folly of incremental change, rather than the wisdom of building new. This is constantly adding new technology to make up for a rotten core. If a large grocery retailer like Tesco were to be built today, it would have an interesting choice. Does it even construct stores around the country and have a super-efficient online unit? Or does it bypass this altogether and be more like Ocado, with automated warehouses? Such a retailer would never deliver items to stores, but would only have people put out stock, then pick it and transport it to people directly. This is the difference between *digital transformation*, building with technology at the core, and *digitalization*, adding some tech on the edge to modernize the system.

When Hertz loses my booking, which is often, I can use a video kiosk to phone up a call centre to complain. They get to see in 4K resolution quite how furious I am. If Hertz were to digitally transform, they'd look more like Zipcar or Uber. In the USA, cheques are still widely used and rather liked. Many US banks have realized how hard it would be to reinvent the financial institutions built on the foundations of the past. So, to make it easier, cheques can now be photographed and deposited via an app. This is the clearest example of merely sprinkling a contemporary digital interface on an archaic broken process. These cheques still cost a fortune and take many days for the bank to process, fraud is an ever-increasing problem and the whole system is wildly inefficient and just doesn't make sense.

So as we seek ways in which companies can best approach today's challenges and opportunities to maximize future potential, let's think more about how we can unlock growth.

It's fun to compare companies and industries that have embraced new realities and models with those that have not. Those who seem very excited about new technology and those who appear reluctant. Those who are rebuilding and reinventing and those who are remaking. Those who are happy to take steps backwards in order to move forward and those who want to build on foundations that just won't support the future. We've learned the importance of depth in bringing about new growth and greater efficiencies. Now we should consider structure, timing, culture and other operational aspects.

Create new value propositions

Value is different in the digital age. I use a slower more expensive train to visit my parents in the UK because it's got fast Wi-Fi and plug sockets. The best thing an Audi owner told me recently about their car is the app you can use to arrange the repair of scratches. I now favour Delta over American Airlines because their app tells you when the flight boards. Not many companies are thinking this way. In the USA I'd happily eschew credit card providers' generous offers of air miles, speedy boarding and free bags on planes, for something that would cost a card issuer $1, a card that lets me pay with contactless. My time is most valuable. I would now choose a bank if it stored all my receipts digitally, I'd choose a car-riding service if it uploaded my receipts for faster expense processing. Value looks different in the modern age.

Reference

Meixler, E (2017) IKEA furniture is about to get easier to buy than ever, *Fortune*, 10 October, available from: http://fortune.com/2017/10/10/ikea-third-party-websites-selling/ [last accessed 7 December 2017]

06
Starting your disruption

Question everything generally thought to be obvious.
RAMS, 1980

For all the talk of change in the business world, you see remarkably little actual change appearing.

In Asia it's different, especially China. Here, it's not so much that they have changed, but more that they have constructed businesses for the first time in the new world. Here we see an abundance of mobile first thinking, common design around digital wallets, companies leveraging the power of instant messaging, QR codes and contemporary logistics that you can build when you have nothing to destroy first. But outside of these markets little has really changed.

As I said earlier, the changes we notice are the most visual and the easiest to do, a sort of MTV *Pimp my Ride* approach to digital transformation. A show in which, while the car owner really needs a new, sensibly priced family car to get around, the producers insist on taking a structurally flawed, mechanically dubious vehicle, gluing it together with paint and putting on wheels so shiny you can't see the smoke bellowing from the exhaust. It makes great TV, but it's a terrible way to change a company.

Now that we've seen the turbulence in the world, and appreciated how businesses can rebuild for the digital age and with new thinking at the core, it's time to plot a path for change. Do we want to continue the slow steady slide to obsolescence, to be the frog that boiled to death, or do we want to be the one that took the brave path to change?

In this chapter, I'll start to outline some of the fundamental questions to be asked, before giving guidance on initial steps to follow. This chapter will be about building a platform for change, establishing core beliefs and values. Chapter 7 then builds in more detail on how companies can practically make it happen.

We need to establish a broader base from which to work, outline a more holistic strategy and take the time now to ask the fundamental and awkward questions.

What is your risk level?

Most people in life are, by human nature, risk averse. We have evolved as a species to reduce losses not maximize gains. We are most driven by the need to avoid humiliation, more than by the need to be the standout winner. There are only two things that both people and companies hate most: when things don't change and when they do. So we need to establish early on, in an era that is chaotic, changes fast and in unpredictable ways, what is your level of personal risk? Do you want to go down in flames as the hero for some (but the fool to others), or do you want to tread carefully like most people do?

Ron Johnson, the ex-senior vice president of retail operations at Apple, was selected to be the CEO of JC Penney. He made bold choices, tried to rewire the company significantly, he was potentially on the verge of great things, but the board threw him out before the moment when these changes could have changed the fortunes of the company forever. In that time the share price fell 50 per cent. So do you see him as a fool or as the kind of charismatic bold leader the world needs?

Real change takes time and involves a lot of hard decisions. It's rebuilding ancient IT systems, firing people who don't want to come along for the ride, establishing new criteria for hiring people, new pay and reward structures. It involves speaking and listening endlessly to customers, auditing all aspects of a company and preparing them for change. It's not a trip to DJI in Shenzhen where you play with drones; it's talking about back ends and protocols. It's not as much fun as a day trip to an innovation lab would suggest and it makes you feel vulnerable.

How vital is this change?

Waves of change are indeed sweeping the world; music and news have suffered, magazines seem on an inevitable path to death, the automotive sector is about to undergo huge shifts as electrical propulsion changes more than would first appear, and new business models proliferate. But it's important to note to what extent *your* business must change. If you are a consumer packaged goods company, then Dollar Shave Club shows what can in theory happen. However, while it was bought for a billion dollars by Unilever, it only threatened to remove value from the market while it was aiming to be acquired; it didn't necessarily change the market as much as trends presentations and over-excited articles suggested.

There is changing because you have to, and there is the opportunity cost of not changing. What is the risk of not changing? Banks may be strong, stable companies that are not forced to change – they can probably buy most start-ups who get interesting and dangerous enough to threaten their business – but wouldn't it be wise to be in control of your own destiny?

Even companies that don't have to change have a lot to gain from change. People are more likely to get divorced than change their bank, even though banks offer all sorts of incentives to move, and yet Monzo Bank in the UK has 40,000 people on a waiting list (Martin, 2017). This is the power of a new clear proposition and of a customer-centric service. When you take on large legacy companies, especially those that are not loved, when you are clear in being an alternative, whether commercially or philosophically, then people will either love you or hate you. This is a powerful emotion and tension to unlock. We would all do well in business to be hyper-aware of what has changed, but even more, remind ourselves frequently of what has stubbornly not changed.

If you are a large legal firm, then yes, you would be wise to employ best-in-class IT staff, to leverage cloud-based software solutions and try out Slack. Legal firms can make heaps of money advising on changes to intellectual property or patent laws, or new disrupted threats, but your business isn't likely to be destroyed by artificial intelligence (AI), robots, or freelance platforms like Upwork; it's likely to be augmented by them. From teaching to general healthcare workers, from dentists to firefighters, there are many industries not facing clear and massive dangers from not changing.

Yet a lot of us really need to wake up. Many of us, and I mean many of us, have our heads in the sand. If you work in the real estate, automotive or insurance markets, big changes are coming. If you are a department store, talent manager or a toy maker, you need to look out. If you write code, you need to be alert to the fact that you are soon likely to be training computers how to do your job and they will self-improve faster than many ever expected. There are many roles like accountants or executive assistants or anyone in media that face pretty big changes ahead. Sectors such as higher education have so far been rather immune to disruption; they've used societal norms to feel confident that things won't ever shift. They probably won't in the near future, but in a world with free information online, where reputations can be built on LinkedIn or by forming your own company, or writing posts that go viral, things seem different. I can learn more from a month on Twitter with a well-curated feed than I did on a four-year master's degree course.

It is up to everyone at this moment in time to look ahead and to establish an understanding of the degree to which you need to change, decisions about whether changing is mandatory, unnecessary or a helpful way to bring an abundance of opportunities your way.

Establishing a role

It is human nature to get small when times feel threatening. It is natural to focus on core activities and cut costs when things look bad. Yet by looking at the role of your company, the value it adds, the brand, and the permission it has to operate in customers' lives, it may be possible to do more. You must consider not only your company's need to change, but also the real opportunity in changing. What business are you really in? Fashions have always come and gone, but if you make athletic clothing, life doesn't seem that different. Yet if you think about things more expansively, if you reconsider your role, things get more interesting and optimistic. If you are a wellness company, you can suddenly do a lot more.

When Harvard marketing professor Theodore Levitt said to his students, 'People don't want to buy a quarter-inch drill. They want a quarter-inch hole', we started to think about products and marketing in new ways (Christensen *et al*, 2005). Clayton Christensen famously took this further with his 'Jobs to be done' framework (Christensen *et al*, 2016). The idea here was that we are not so much in the business of selling items, drills, milkshakes, or new watches but are actually trying to accomplish something more bold and ambitious.

Marketing experts do a great job of trying to elevate the role of a company and product. Pepsi, for example, is touted as being a solution to racism, or violence, while Coca-Cola just settles for owning the entire concept of happiness, globally. Some tangy chocolate cookies go from standing for 'crunchy and tasty' to 'satisfying hunger' to 'celebrating world peace' in about three meetings with advertising agency strategists.

But the truth is there is much to be said for standing for something greater, particularly when it comes to promoting transformation and innovation.

Hyatt, Holiday Inn and Starwood hotels are in the business of making and running world-class hotels, which is a great business to be in, but it limits these companies. In this model of thinking, they need total control over the management of the property. It means they are totally to blame for any problems that arise: no rooms available, dirty service areas, it's all tarnishing the brand and not the property owner. Quality control issues limit the speed at which you can expand, the areas that are profitable to enter, the liability you face rises the more you control.

Airbnb challenged this. Initially, it stood for 'a roof over your head' regardless of how it was delivered, with first an 'AIRmattress and Bed And Breakfast' and later, more proper beds and fewer breakfasts. The platform can now grow in two very interesting horizontal directions: it can stand for humanity and the idea of 'people helping people', which allows it to run tours (as it has started to do); but also offers potential future expansion into anything about people that requires trust, such as casual jobs, food preparation, ride-shares. The business can be propelled in any direction that requires a reputation online and the codification of trust. 'What's empowered this shift in values is the codification of reputation – it's the five stars next to people's names that make it possible to trust someone we otherwise know nothing about' (Stan, 2016).

And it could also move vertically, It could branch out into the 'housing' arena, building (or leasing out its name) to liveable hotels, friendly-feeling apartments, murphy beds, and interior design. Airbnb has the potential to stand for anything in the horizontal or vertical. That's quite something.

Thinking about the role your business plays in people's lives is a big way to grow. The roles of many incumbents are under threat and this is the core issue. Why do we need department stores at a time when we can see everything we love online? Living in a small city in 1980 they made sense. Someone gathered a selection of good things together, then arranged them nicely to showcase for me, but in the modern age this has no value; we don't need a bundler. So from car rental firms to department stores, from record labels to magazine brands, how can we re-imagine the role we have? Perhaps department stores need to become 'advisors' for fashion, health and life, perhaps magazines need to become lifestyle brands that run hotels and exclusive parties.

When we think of it this way, life becomes exciting for many. Gyms are not places you pay money to each month in order to access their space and machines; they become holistic lifestyle organizations that can help you attain any goal. The gym becomes less about a nice big room and clean mirror and the latest equipment, and more about fitness tracking with apps, access to wellness coaches and nutritionists, places that can make money in new ways, affiliate marketing for live insurance, spa break holidays. Gyms could own our health and wellness.

Banks can stand for being the gateway to spending, saving, all the bills we pay. They can go from being places to trust with our savings, to being the guardians and advisors on financial health. Mobile operators around the world are terrified about being 'dumb pipes'. How can they leverage the relationship they have with all of us and our billing details, and become owners of content, managers of mobile payments, advisors in our relationship with data and news?

The steps to think about here are: realistically, what role can you have in your audience's life? What do you have credibility to do?

How deep can it go? Do you have permission to do this? I don't think a tea company can own social networks, despite its social roots, but I think a car company can stand for mobility, an airline can represent leisure, and a home improvement store can represent interior design and architecture. There is no reason IKEA or Muji can't sell homes.

Establishing a time to change

Where were you when you got your very first bar of 3G reception? One of the worst first-date questions you can ever ask, but for me it was memorable. It was early 2007, and I was high in the Durmitor mountain range in Montenegro. As the rusty train meandered past medieval villages and creakily zigzagged its way through derelict train stations, I was quickly e-mailing images of the previous night's disgusting meal I'd had in a burnt-out train station. Progress happens in unexpected ways.

We've all been there. You've been wanting a new games console for ages and the week you buy it they bring out a new one. Well, just imagine you're a car company that just spent $100 million on a new engine plant, just as electric propulsion looks to be the future. Or you've just bought Blackberries for all your staff, or committed to bringing back coal jobs. Sometimes the future happens so fast it's hard to know when to take the leap.

We see brand new planes with no power outlets – whoops, someone didn't think. You ride high-speed train lines costing billions that nobody thought to put Wi-Fi in. New roads with manned toll booths. It's amazing to travel to countries where they built for the new world from nothing. You can pay by text for parking in Romania, because they didn't need meters in the communist age. TeliaSonera was the first operator in the world to commercially launch 4G cellular systems in late 2009, in Lithuania. Some of the fastest internet speeds in the world are in Estonia. China now accounts for as much as 70 per cent of the world's total installed solar thermal capacity.

New technology is always better in ways we can't imagine. In New York City, when I watch TV in my apartment, I watch it via a huge cable box, I get standard HD resolution and a choice of 200 channels for $120 per month. Yet whip out my iPhone 7, 45 times smaller and 16 times lighter than my cable box, use it as a hotspot and I can stream video from anywhere in the world, at four times greater resolution via 4G and my Apple TV. It's amazing how the latest technology can be orders of magnitude better. It's incredibly exciting to witness the progress that this sort of leapfrogging allows.

Villages in Africa can in theory equip themselves not with expensive-to-build, hard-to-maintain, slow-to-stock libraries, but could hand out $10 smartphones and tablets and let kids learn how to do anything. An underdeveloped nation like Tanzania will officially kick off the world's largest delivery drone service in 2018 (Walcutt, 2017). Who needs roads any more?

Four ways to change

When you know what you are about to do, what you can reach for, what market you can be part of, you can then think about how deeply you must change, and ponder one of four ways to change.

There are many ways to change your business. It is a sliding scale; there is no point at which a company that is putting a big effort into buying new and non-core businesses is suddenly a company that is re-engineering itself. How much do you have to invest in start-ups before it goes from being a nice way to outsource research & development and maximize learnings, to becoming a hedging strategy for the future of the business? So, these ways do not have clear boundaries, but I think in each case it should be fairly clear what approach is being taken when I give examples.

1 Self-disruption

By far the riskiest, most aggressive, most potentially rewarding approach towards change is to self-disrupt. There are two clear elements that define self-disruption vs any other form of wholesale change.

Firstly, self-disruption has to involve a degree of cannibalism. The driving force behind self-disruption is to create a business that first wins market share and gains new customers, but ultimately should become so large and successful that it becomes the driving factor in the future of the company itself. The goal is to create an entity that challenges so many industry norms, becomes such a valuable and clear consumer proposition, that at some point it's likely to be more successful than the original company. While in an ideal world both entities, the legacy unit and the thrusting start-up, would survive, there will always be a risk of cannibalism. To some extent, assuming the companies are in the same general industry, the more successful the start-up becomes, by definition the more it's likely to eat its parent. It's the degree of risk and sacrifice in this model that is key.

It's easier to define the idea with examples of what it's not.

When British Airways set up Go, they were not doing so because they wanted the whole airline to become a low-cost carrier and give up on premium passengers. They did it reluctantly and defensively because of a threat from low-cost carriers.

When the Inditex Group, most famously known for the Zara brand, decided to open a premium fashion retailer, Massimo Dutti, in 1985, while it was ambitious enough to want to own a premium market and increase profitability, it was never expected to eat the parent brand of Zara and become the future of the company. Both British Airways and Inditex are just portfolio approaches to brands from parent companies.

Secondly, self-disruption is rooted in the notion of acting fast, early and, most importantly, before you have to. If you buy a competitor that's rapidly eating your market share and ride on the back of it, this is merely a sensible acquisition strategy. It's investing, as most companies would, in protecting their position. What is key about self-disruption is that you act before many think you have to.

In 2014, when Facebook bought WhatsApp for $19 billion (BBC, 2014), it did so because the company was a threat to the success of its own messaging platform, and ultimately its own company, but it did so less as a proactive and aggressive play, and more as a defensive move.

When Walmart bought Jet.com for $3.3 billion in 2016 (Reuters, 2016), it was less about confidently and positively creating its own future; it was the acceptance that it didn't have the right skills, size and reputation in the online marketplace to compete with Amazon.

It's worth adding that it is these defensive moves by large legacy players that fuel a huge proportion of venture capital investments. Most mobile-based 'banks of the future' are basically created to be irritating, dangerous, large and attractive enough so they will be bought by an incumbent business that realizes it is too late to start its own.

Many of these companies are like pacemakers in long-distance running; they can't make the entire distance but that's not what they are there for. Sometimes they get so far ahead that, perhaps even surprisingly to the founders, they end up winning. It's possible to see Netflix and Tesla in this light.

There are very few examples of self-disruption. Large legacy players are often too big, too reluctant to accept they are not right, too careful not to signal to the financial markets that they are somehow not already the best placed company to survive. This way of changing is more likely to be used by smaller companies, ones with more to gain, yet often the smaller size of these entities makes them feel too vulnerable to pursue this course.

Self-disruption is like seeing a therapist when most patients would rather have a boob job. Taking those first steps can sometimes feel like steps backwards; it is mentally hard and most people want faster results.

In two years of research the best example of self-disruption I can find is Netflix.

Netflix's transition to streaming from DVD rental by mail was not nearly as smooth as many would like to remember it, but in hindsight it appears genius.

Netflix was founded in 1997 as a DVD mail service and pretty rapidly rose to take huge market share from local video stores who could not compete with its vast range of titles. People soon appreciated the appeal of no late fees, the ability to have several movies out at the same time, as well as its unlimited consumption tariff.

Always keen to keep abreast of the latest technology, in 2007 Netflix spent about $40 million to build data centres and to cover the cost of licensing for the initial streaming titles (Rodriguez, 2017). When internet speeds allowed, it introduced streaming as an additional service for its existing subscribers. Monthly fees remained the same, but those with more expensive tariffs were given access to more hours of streamed content. While it added something for free, it also helped give people a reason to upgrade to more expensive plans. Growth was impressive, the video libraries of streamed content rose, the share price rose impressively from $3 in 2007 to over $42 in 2011, and life was good.

In September 2011 Netflix made a very bold move. It created two tariffs, and moved all its US subscribers onto two separate plans: the original DVD-by-mail service was to be called Qwikster; the other was a streaming service for a lower monthly fee. The market was shocked, and by December the stock price was below $10 and the company was in pieces. The company rapidly lost higher revenue DVD subscribers and within nine months profits were down by 50 per cent (Steel, 2015).

And yet slowly things changed. First, the lower prices suddenly appealed to a much wider market, bringing in far more paying customers, allowing Netflix to buy more content and to slowly raise prices. Then Netflix started making its own original content, clearing out global streaming rights, and then at a flick of a switch it was able to expand globally.

If Netflix had not disrupted itself it would be a very different company. It would rely on a massive physical distortion system, with very high costs. It would probably have lost out massively to YouTube and would have withered away as a mail-order DVD supplier.

Instead, Netflix's share price is now nearly $200, five times more than it was when it bravely self-disrupted, it operates in 190 countries, makes nearly $9 billion in revenue from over 110 million customers (Feldman, 2017). Today DVDs represent only 4 per cent of Netflix's users. It seems that in 2011, when Wall Street was demanding the resignation of Reed Hastings for reinventing the business, they were wrong.

From this you can see the pressure this approach places on leaderships, the confidence you need to have, the degree to which this antagonizes the market and everyone around you. This move takes balls. The confidence, conviction, and aggression, to change before you have to create your own future, is remarkable.

It's why it rarely happens. IAC is a media and internet group, one of whose brands is the online dating Match Group. Figure 6.1 shows

Figure 6.1 Match Group mobile dating apps: US market share by session, January 2013 to November 2014

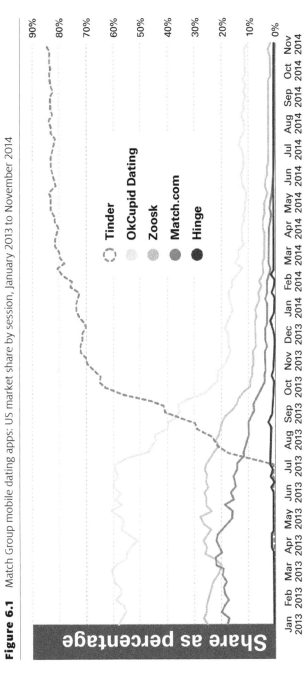

SOURCE 7 Park Data, http://www.businessinsider.com/jmp-securities-analyst-note-on-tinder-2015-4

the US market shares of IAC's Match Group portfolio, which includes online dating sites Match.com, OKCupid etc. Match went on to create Tinder in what can be seen as a form of self-disruption: a free dating site that was once massively undermining the user numbers and profitability of the company's own dating sites. Tinder was launched before it had to and under no competitive pressure, and it was incubated under Hatch Labs, which IAC partly owned.

You could perhaps argue that when the mobile operator O2 launched a far cheaper, youth-focused tariff with the idea of it being 'mutual, simple and fair', it was cannibalistic enough to be self-disruptive, but I don't think the ambition was there.

When Amazon launched the Kindle, a device that could have in theory displaced a significant portion of its own book sales, on which the company was founded, it happened at a point when the company was making more money in other ways.

Self-disruption may not be right for you. Is the baby so bad you need to throw it out with the bathwater? For some companies, lurching confidently into the future is vital. I'd not want to be in the department store or magazine printing business much longer, but most companies can approach self-disruption more positively. They don't have to eat the old entity soon, they don't need to assume that the new unit won't take far more from other competitors and be accretive. For most companies, there is an urgent need to set up new future-focused units or buy units that lead to growth but that don't bring with them the risk of self-destruction. These I introduce in the next section.

2 Continual reinvention

At what point does a start-up become a legacy business? Are eBay or Skype or Microsoft examples of some of the world's oldest start-ups or of the youngest legacy businesses? To some extent the transition seems to occur when they go from being the hunter to being the hunted, from pursuing growth to maintaining profitability, from offence to defence.

Continual reinvention is a profound and serious commitment to change and at the deepest levels, one based in the idea that the best defence is a good offence. It is the process by which companies maintain a significant position in a market, by undertaking continual and significant changes to maintain that position. This process may take various forms.

As I mentioned before, there is no magical line companies cross from being mere significant innovators to being continual reinventors. There is something about the size of these investments, however, and the frequency with which they are core to the business, rather than just buying another form of revenue. American Airlines buying US Airways was a big financial deal, but it wasn't reinvention or acquiring a future threat; it was just a step to become bigger and change little else.

The difference with self-disruption is that there is less risk of cannibalization, it's less proactive and more reactive. When Adobe moved slowly from selling its software on disks to selling its software as perpetual licences to becoming a cloud-based software-as-a-service (SAAS) provider where you merely pay for their Creative Cloud, it represented a great example of continual reinvention, not self-disruption.

Another good example is IBM, a company that first made massive mainframe computers, but which over decades became marginalized by mini-computers. So IBM shifted to the business and consumer personal computer market, before largely giving up on hardware and buying SoftLayer to become an infrastructure-as-a-service provider, then a management consulting outfit, and now is looking to become a leader in AI with IBM Watson.

Continual reinvention always feels like progress. It feels risky, but generally speaking it's undertaken by companies in fast-changing sectors. TV or media owners in theory should have bought Facebook when it was small, they should regret the day Snapchat was born, newspapers should kick themselves for not starting Twitter, but these sectors don't think this way. Recently ASOS became more valuable than long-standing UK high-street leader Marks & Spencer – but you just don't sense that these companies think about change in this way.

It's hard to keep turning companies around, so most examples of this form of innovation have been done through acquisition. Microsoft, to its credit, has invested in maintaining relevance and making big calls.

In a world that loves Apple, we forget that Microsoft is today worth more than ever at $642 billion, and has nearly tripled in value since 2010. In the last five years Microsoft's share price has gone up by 200 per cent, and Apple's 'only' by 114 per cent (Fraley, 2017).

Arguably the best example of this serial investment approach is Facebook. While the company itself spends billions on R&D, it really seems to rely on buying the most promising developments by acquiring thrusting companies who are growing fast, just before they get too successful to resist selling (they missed Snapchat this way) or too expensive.

In 2012, as the web was becoming more visual, as cameras were getting more advanced, as the mobile sharing of images became most popular, Facebook made probably one of their best ever investments: for the at-the-time insanely high price of $1 billion, Facebook bought Instagram. In retrospect this was a genius move that allowed Facebook to dominate imaging. And while some think Instagram is worth $50 billion, many believe that, since so many people are threatening to leave Facebook, Instagram is a safety net worth far more than this, and that in fact it has allowed Facebook to swell from a $58 billion company to a $500+ billion business.

Each and every time a new screen or behaviour appears, Zuckerberg has been quick to pounce. Facebook's need to stay modern, to get the best people, to ensure they don't miss out on the next big thing, has been behind their acquisition of WhatsApp for instant messaging, Oculus for virtual reality, face.com for face recognition, MSQRD for facial filters and swapping, and most recently Ozlo for better driven AI on messaging.

Is continual reinvention right for you? Continual reinvention is based on paranoia and things changing fast and is not for everyone. Samsung doesn't need to assume that everyone is a threat to their refrigerator business and buy everyone in that space. Nike does not need to panic about Allbirds and set about buying everyone that dares make shoes. For companies that are faddish in nature, that don't offer much in the way of protective moats, for companies in spaces growing fast, this makes more sense. Perhaps a TV station should be buying a fast-growing video site, perhaps Lyft should acquire Gett, or Wal-Mart buy ASOS, but it's not for everyone. Some need a calmer approach.

3 Measured bets

The most common approach to innovation is one that is far less involved, less deeply integrated, and typically not part of a long-term, continuous approach to innovation. Sometimes these approaches are bolder and bigger, and more threatening to the parent company; other times they are clearly small offshoots, less likely to have a strong chance to change the future, and are more about testing the market, learning more about the business environment, or just showing the world they can do it.

Midland Bank (now part of HSBC) was probably the first company ever to do 'a start-up' when they set up First Direct. Created in 1989 from the need to find new growth, especially from profitable, reliable, affluent customers, First Direct started life as a blank sheet of paper with the word 'customer' in the middle. Inspired and intrigued by the idea of telephone banking, an entirely new company was created from nothing, but was based on the notion of reinventing everything in the banking model. They destroyed all conventions in the industry: the bank would be open 24 hours a day, would have no bank service charges, would deliver helpful unbureaucratic, unfussy, customer-oriented service. It seemed to change the world of banking overnight, and for the first time ever, a bank seemed fresh, modern and different. People loved banking with First Direct.

First Direct has been in profit every year since 1995, more than one in three of First Direct's customers join because of personal recommendation, and they have over 1.3 million customers (First Direct, 2010).

The BMW i is a sub-brand of BMW founded in 2011 to manufacture plug-in electric vehicles. It's part sub-brand and part innovation lab for the main parent company. So far two BMW i models have been made: the surprisingly practical i3 all-electric car and the i8 plug-in hybrid. BMW i series is now sold in 50 countries. While the unit itself has sold over 100,000 cars, it's unlikely to be close to being profitable by itself. Instead, the company is a feeder unit to the main company, developing technology to be used in other cars. In fact, in 2017, BMW confirmed that by 2025 it will sell 25 electrified vehicles, nearly half of which will be purely electric (Taylor and Preisenger,

2017). It's this example which shows how innovation can be done both internally and significantly but without threatening the main corporate brand, and with the hope that, one day, the two will blend.

Measured bets are what most companies do. It's just that some are smaller than others. However, I worry that measured bets are too small. It's PR not corporate strategy. Companies need to get bolder with how they place bets on change. The process needs to be much more about core change, not just the superficial. The fourth and final approach derives from even less ambition to change, and more from the need to spread risk.

4 Hedge fund

A significant and increasing number of companies think that their future is best placed in the hands of others. Perhaps you think turning your company round yourself is just too hard, or that achieving growth by investing in other businesses, just as a private investor would with a share portfolio, is a sensible use of your company assets. We are seeing the growth of well-funded, high-revenue-earning companies that do not seek to buy, take over or run interesting companies, but instead invest heavily in them so that they can share in their success, often without any controlling stake or seats on the board.

This is not a new concept. In 1914, the president of chemical and plastics manufacturer DuPont, Pierre du Pont, invested in the then still private and only six-year-old car company called General Motors.

Corporate hedging is done with an independent arm of a company or a designated investment team, off their company's balance sheet. The goal is to invest in high-growth companies that drive value for the company. Companies like Google Ventures and equivalents from Cisco, Intel, or Dell have been using this approach for some time. It's been common for technology companies to do this.

The most dramatic example of all comes from the huge Japanese mobile carrier, Softbank. It's already a holding company with self-driving cars, energy trading units and cloud services, yet now it's leading a new fund, called the Vision Fund. It's raised $93 billion to do it, putting only $28 billion of its own money into it (Massoudi *et al*, 2017).

I am not aware of any company that has tried to change too much, too quickly. I don't see any examples of companies taking this too seriously. I see small bets placed, I see innovation labs that open and do nothing, I see PR stunts and I see the gesture of change. Not everything is changing, not everything will change, but I'd like to see companies get more excited about what is made easier, faster, better, cheaper, and more popular every day. I'd like to see hotels delight in what they could do extra, retailers embrace the power of influencers, car companies get excited about what it would be like to thrill customers with a sense of belonging. Let's start to consider what more practical things companies can do to achieve this.

In this chapter, we've explored how to establish a base to grow from, how you can alter remuneration strategy to incentivize people to bring about long-term change, how you can drive a platform for change, and think about the role you will play in consumers' lives in a more expansive way. But once you've done that, what can you actually do to bring about change? This is what I explore in the next chapter.

References

BBC (2014) Facebook to buy messaging app WhatsApp for $19bn, 20 February, available from: http://www.bbc.co.uk/news/business-26266689 [last accessed 7 December 2017]

Christensen, CM, Cook, S and Hall, T (2005) Marketing malpractice: The cause and the cure, *Harvard Business Review,* 83(12), December 2005

Christensen, CM, Hall, T, Dillon, K and Duncan, DS (2016) Know your customers' 'jobs to be done', *Harvard Business Review,* September 2016, available from: https://hbr.org/2016/09/know-your-customers-jobs-to-be-done [last accessed 7 December 2017]

Feldman, D (2017) Netflix is on track to exceed $11bn in revenue this year, *Forbes,* 16 October, available from: https://www.forbes.com/sites/danafeldman/2017/10/16/netflix-is-on-track-to-exceed-11b-in-revenue-this-year/#417ac27b65dd [last accessed 7 December 2017]

First Direct (2010) First Direct turns 21 – 21 facts about the UK's most customer friendly bank [online] available from: https://www.newsroom.firstdirect.com/press/release/first_direct_turns_21_-_21_fac [last accessed 7 December 2017]

Fraley, C (2017) Why Microsoft Corporation stock is more reliable than Apple Inc. stock, *Investor Place*, 27 November, available from: https://investorplace.com/2017/11/msft-stock-more-reliable/#.WikoMmXPyEI [last accessed 7 December 2017]

Martin, C (2017) What is Monzo Bank, *Tech Advisor*, 17 October, available from: https://www.techadvisor.co.uk/buying-advice/gadget/what-is-mondo-bank-3644615/ [last accessed 7 December 2017]

Massoudi, A, Inagaki, K and Hook, L (2017) SoftBank's Son uses rare structure for $93bn tech fund, *Financial Times*, 12 June, available from: https://www.ft.com/content/b6fe313a-4add-11e7-a3f4-c742b9791d43 [last accessed 7 December 2017]

Rams, D (1980) Speech to Braun Supervisory Board, Design Museum, available at: http://designmuseum.org/design/dieter-rams [last accessed 7 December 2017]

Reuters (2016) Walmart has completed its acquisition of Jet.com, *Fortune*, 20 September, available from: http://fortune.com/2016/09/20/walmart-acquisition-jetcom/ [last accessed 7 December 2017]

Rodriguez, M (2017) Ten years ago, Netflix launched streaming video and changed the way we watch everything, *Quartz*, 17 January, available from: https://qz.com/887010/netflix-nflx-launched-streaming-video-10-years-ago-and-changed-the-way-we-watch-everything/ [last accessed 7 December 2017]

Stan, A (2016) The future is the trust economy, TechCrunch, 24 April, available from: https://techcrunch.com/2016/04/24/the-future-is-the-trust-economy/ [last accessed 7 December 2017]

Steel, E (2015) Netflix profits slide 50% as streaming growth lags, *The New York Times* [online], 14 October, available from: https://www.nytimes.com/2015/10/15/business/media/netflix-3q-earnings.html [last accessed 7 December 2017]

Taylor, E and Preisenger, I (2017) BMW gears up to mass produce electric cars by 2020, Reuters, 7 September, available from: https://www.reuters.com/article/us-autoshow-frankfurt/bmw-gears-up-to-mass-produce-electric-cars-by-2020-idUSKCN1BI1LM [last accessed 7 December 2017]

Walcutt, L (2017) Zipline is launching the world's largest drone delivery network in Tanzania, *Forbes*, 24 August, available from: https://www.forbes.com/sites/leifwalcutt/2017/08/24/zipline-is-launching-the-worlds-largest-drone-delivery-network-in-tanzania/#763a794a293b [last accessed 7 December 2017]

07
Today's business dynamics

The secret of change is to focus all of your energy, not on fighting the old, but on building the new.
MILLMAN, 1980

Few people expect to get a glimpse of the future in Slough. But the drab corridors of the town's Crowne Plaza Hotel contrasted sharply with the profound insight into the future I received there.

It was 2006, and I was working with the Nokia Nseries marketing team. We were holding focus groups with prototype touchscreen phones, the like of which nobody had ever seen before. This was way before the iPhone. It was fair to say that not everyone saw the future that day. People almost without exception hated the new phones. They worried that the screens would smash even though we assured them that they would not. They hated the fact that the battery life was less than two days. They worried about strange things such as fingerprints making the screen greasy. Above all else, people couldn't really see the point. For the outrageous trade-offs that had to be made – the large screen necessary to view photos that people were yet to share and to access apps that didn't yet exist – the main takeaway was that it did more than they needed to. I remember more than anything else the proclamation that, 'I like the internet, but I've already got it at home'.

Even those companies who see the future more than most can find it very hard to change.

In this chapter I want to outline how to build on the foundation of change I introduced in Chapter 6. Regardless of whether you are changing all or very little, how can we bring about the changes to any business that will help drive enthusiasm for new technology, passion for change, and a positive feeling about growth?

These are exciting times. We forget that. It seems today that it's easier to set up a large media company like Vice, Quartz or the Outline from nothing than it is to rewire a legacy business to become one. It seems as if it's easier to set up a brand like Glossier or e.l.f. from scratch than to get Estée Lauder or Beiersdorf to make it. This should feel like good news for everyone, but it rarely does.

In this chapter, we will explore why companies have so far failed to innovate, in order that we can understand their reasons and offer suggestions for how they can innovate in future. How can they combine the best of both legacy knowledge, which includes industry recognition and expertise, with the need to embrace what's now possible?

So why don't big companies innovate?

Blue Bottle Coffee is one of the many success stories of 2017, recently valued at $700 million after meteoric growth for 15 years (Atkins and Bradshaw, 2017). It's the sort of company that sets the tone for the start-up scene and creates the role model every start-up owner wants to become. If you wanted to start Blue Bottle Coffee today, it would require a lot of effort and not insignificant resources.

You'd want a team that understood branding and could develop a great image for the coffee. You'd ideally have access to the best ad agencies in the world and the best graphic designers. Ideally, you'd have some sort of food engineers to perfect the product, to hone over months the perfect flavour profile and the right way to store and mix products. You'd want some analytics and insights staff to see trends ahead. You'd want packaging experts owning relationships with packing companies, alongside procurement and sourcing people holding the skills to find the best products on earth and the power to negotiate down price. You might also want a real estate expert, and a good legal team. Now armed with all this expertise, you would need cash behind you. Perhaps you may need $20 million to start with enough potential. It's a pretty pure combination of branding, building and design.

You might imagine that the sort of company that would be well placed to do this may be Procter & Gamble with their marketing prowess and deep pockets, or maybe Mondalez with their food experience and huge global footprint, or perhaps Nestlé, whose R&D budget is estimated at around $1.7 billion per year (YCharts, 2017). It's pretty clear that all these companies were ideally placed to create Blue Bottle, but none of them did.

Blue Bottle was started by a self-proclaimed 'coffee lunatic' called James Freeman, who in 2002 decided to start selling his roasted coffee beans at a farmers' market in Oakland, California. He used the buy-out money he received from being an early employee at a pre-Pandora start-up. Until 2008 (when he took on a minority investor), his business had survived on very little money, with Freeman putting in just $15,000 and taking on some credit card debt to launch his company.

In total, by early 2015 the company had taken about $45 million in funding (Sacks, 2014). In 2017, Nestlé spent $500 million to acquire 68 per cent of Blue Bottle – a brand and company it could have easily built itself (Atkins and Bradshaw, 2017).

Buying innovation is the fashion

This strange behaviour is everywhere right now. When Unilever bought Dollar Shave Club for $1 billion (Primack, 2016), it didn't get any patents, an R&D team or a production facility. There were no valuable commercial deals, or amazing staff to acquihire (buying a company in order to recruit the staff). It was just 190 employees who made a thin veneer of a company that resold Dorco generic razor blades, via a logistics company in Kentucky (both of whom made money) while Dollar Shave Club lost money on every order and every customer.

Again, regardless of whether the deal was good or not, the fact remains: why could they have not done this themselves?

Accounting and outsourcing risk

I've asked a few of these companies and companies like them in similar circumstances and I learned a lot. I was always there for 'innovation days', days to be out of the office, forget about the real job, and to dream big. Sitting in the room, it always felt to me that at best it was like teaching art in school, where people would look forward to it, and love it, but mainly because it didn't matter. At worst it would feel like a sort of adult crèche, a way to keep people busy and take some nice photos. We'd have post-it notes and coloured sofas, boards with 'dream big' and motivational quotes. Probably a story from a founder and a fashion blogger shipped in to talk about the spirit of innovation and someone else to talk about passion. It was always very sanitized. Being me, I would frequently get quite cross and ask these people the annoying questions, like 'why didn't *you* create these companies?'.

For one thing, the accounting procedures killed innovation. Most FMCG companies are factories with marketing departments stuck on the side. Procurement plays a major role, and much like staples, sugar, or ammonium chloride, everything that costs money is measured, the cost of it driven down and real needs established. Now it's bad enough buying ideas or advertising in a procurement-driven culture, but when buying innovation it is crippling.

By definition innovation is something new. There is no return on investment (ROI). There is no meaningful ROI possible for anything bold and new. What was the Wright Brothers' ROI for flying? In 1985, what was the ROI for inventing Red Bull? What customer research showed people wanted bagless vacuum cleaners? If you can't show an ROI, about the only other thing you can do to get investment signed off is to show case studies of what your competitors have done, and use their actions to justify yours. It's by this reckoning that Tropicana can make smoothies but only after Innocent owned the market, or large European car companies can make electric cars, but only very late in the day.

Big companies are about continuous improvement, about making everything slightly better, slightly cheaper, each and every year. They wait for start-ups to get big, pull out a billion dollars or so, buy the company, and get to showcase to the world that they are ambitious, financially strong, that they get the change. The cost of this unit goes straight to the balance sheet as an asset for the price paid, the share price may go up by more than this, life is good. Why would anyone have it any other way? How about because it's a very inefficient way to change and there is a long predictable history of large companies failing to work well with what they've bought. Something needs to change.

Establishing a leadership for change

The reality is that many CEOs and leaders don't actually want to change. They have it too good. John Winsor, the founder of Victor and Spoils and long-time innovation leader, believes a lack of real change 'comes down to misaligned incentives' in what he labels the 'Hamptons Effect' (Winsor, 2017). It is this incorrect alignment of the best interests of the company and the best interests of the leadership that is the big force stopping change. Looked at objectively, many people could actually be regarded as smart for not wanting change.

Typical CEOs are not trying to make their career, they're trying to round it off. He (because invariably it is a he) isn't trying to make a name, he's not wanting to be the one that brought about change. For the majority of CEOs the allure of a steady retirement, playing golf and a step change after a hard career is naturally very strong.

Short-termism is killing ambition

Short-term thinking is everywhere and it makes radical change and investing in the future very hard. In 1940 the average period a share was held was seven years and for around 35 years this changed little. By the 1987 crash, stocks were held for less than two years, by 2007 this had fallen to seven months, and today it's four months. And that's if you ignore high-frequency trading, where the typical hold plummets to 11 seconds (Haldane, 2010).

Everything in the business world seems to be accelerating. The average tenure of a CEO is now 6.6 years, compared to 8.1 years a decade ago (Weinmann and Groth, 2011). Today leadership roles are primarily facing the financial markets. Every public company is led by CEOs, leadership teams, and departmental managers, whose entire financial future is held hostage by the share price. It's this condition that means all decisions must be made with regard to credit brokers, stock market analysts, stock pickers, journalists.

One would assume companies would pray at the altar that is customer service, or better products, or designing great experiences, but in fact most corporate entities entirely face Wall Street in the USA, the City in London and their equivalents around the world.

It means news must be managed, risks must be avoided, balance sheets must be guarded. Numbers must be reported quarterly, profit warnings given where appropriate. Companies with stature and history are forced to show continuing profits, maintain the vital price-to-earnings ratio, keep the EBITDA (earnings before interest, taxes, depreciation and amortization) and maintain dividend payments to investors to keep share prices high.

We need to find a way to change this culture. The wavelength for re-engineering many companies around the level of change they reasonably need is far greater than typical tenures in roles or what the stock market will forgive. The current financial environment only rewards those who cut their way to profitability, not those who invest for growth in the future. We have an especially strange trend where companies can celebrate revenue growth in fields that are unprofitable. 'Look at how many new customers we have online' is a frequent boast, without the acknowledgement that these customers lose us money.

If companies are ever to succeed long term, they need to establish a way to reward those who turned ships around, not who jumped while things looked fine.

Success takes time

It's rather counter-intuitive. We feel that tech companies espouse agility and speed, but the most successful companies today are companies that have operated with the long term in mind. Amazon now spends over \$16 billion in R&D, and Jeff Bezos makes a point of not wanting to turn a profit for a very long term and investing all potential income into growth for the future (Molla, 2017). The tempo of most public companies is set by the three-month beat of quarterly earnings, but the strongest and most fashionable companies have become masters of setting their own tempo.

Strong leaders give the teams and company confidence to manage timelines the best way: sometimes it's the need to be fast and decisive, and other times it's about waiting for the right moment. Often innovation isn't about jumping to things first, it's not about first-mover advantage but knowing when the time is right.

Charismatic leadership

When we look to the companies we most often admire, that have either become successful recently or become textbook examples of how to lead, we notice the rise of the enigmatic and strong-minded leader.

With the right leadership in place, the right mission in mind, with a role and goal in sight, we can then create the key elements needed for a company's prosperous future. What ends up with tactics, products, service and initiatives starts out with leadership that creates a culture for change. However, culture is exactly the thing that can hold innovation back. Culture means ideas are killed early or never shared or most likely are never even born. A lack of innovation in the culture of an organization will reinforce itself: bad talent nurtures talent badly and attracts the same. I'll explore this later and what can be done about it, but first let's focus on how to change culture. It comes from the top.

Strong HR and talent departments can help ensure people work around objectives not around 'busyness'. Too often we celebrate how hard we work, not what we accomplish. Corporate culture today is typically about being in the meeting, not establishing if the meeting really needed to happen. Trust is a vital part of management by objective. It is also vital to ensure that people feel free, empowered, important, relied upon. This combination allows employees to work from wherever they would like to best get their job done, to make sensible decisions, to undertake risky actions but with good intentions and good information and to do so by asking forgiveness if things go wrong, not permission before they act. A strong HR function can empower rogue behaviour, the sort of behaviour most likely to drive growth in new ways.

When wonderful people can work anywhere, companies need to strive to make the most of people. Reward them in strange ways, make happiness the number one goal, allow them to be relaxed and feel valued. They are to some extent all you have.

An intolerance of bureaucracy

Small companies feel different to big ones. I have worked at both. In large companies, if I am travelling for work I will be forced to use some admin staff to book a hotel with a corporate travel provider. Perhaps eight e-mails will be sent to me with various approval chains and updates, my boss will be asked to agree, a business reason is noted. Some systems will talk to others, and my assistant will orchestrate the whole thing. It will take perhaps 10 minutes of my time, 30 minutes of my assistant's, and likely an hour of other people's in back offices. All this to book a hotel stay for $200 that on the Hotel Tonight app I could book in around three seconds and for $100 cheaper. Why is it I can call an hour-long meeting with 20 people, costing perhaps $2,500 of time and nobody cares, but I need to ensure I use approved agents to get a hotel room?

Every company, large and small, needs to reject bureaucracy and busy work. We worry a lot about seniority and protocol, but often it is an excuse. I love a memo sent out by Elon Musk, in which he says: 'Anyone at Tesla can and should e-mail/talk to anyone else according to what they think is the fastest way to solve a problem for the benefit of the whole company. You can talk to your manager's manager without his permission, you can talk directly to a VP in another department, you can talk to me.' He goes on to say, while realizing the challenge and opportunity ahead and what they have against them, 'We obviously cannot compete with the big car companies in size, so we must do so with intelligence and agility' (Bariso, 2017).

Get better at knowing when to call and when to e-mail, when to pop over for a chat, which partner meetings to never accept. A lack of bureaucracy doesn't mean chaos, it's about focusing on the best way to make a difference and sometimes that means anarchically barging into a meeting to get someone to make a decision.

I often think teams are too big. We've long heard about two pizza teams, but let's be more flexible. Tom Peters talks about the need to recruit the very best talent and pay the world's best compensation. Steve Jobs was widely reported to have stated that a small number of A+ people can outperform any large teams of B players (Keller and Meaney, 2017). I see a lot of time and energy spent bringing people into the loop, people being part of things to look important and not adding clear value.

Celebrate failure

I would love to see a key performance indicator as 'the biggest failure' each year and what you've learned from it. If you have not messed up in a rather large way, you've not been pushing hard enough. In the Swedish town of Helsingborg near Stockholm there is a small museum, which, rather than showcasing success – companies, works, designs or artwork that worked – does the opposite. In a world that loves the winners, it celebrates the world's absolute disasters. The Museum of Failure advocates that we should idolize those who tried. Worrying about failure makes us tight, unhappy, uncreative. We need to imbue within all of us a sense of discovery and adventure. Well at least those who have thinking-based roles.

We need to accept imperfection. Good may be the enemy of the great but perfect is the enemy of getting stuff done. There is a vulnerability in many environments if you are to share things that are not quite perfect or perfectly thought through. The idea of presenting a new product without showing reams of research to show that it definitely will work is contrary to how most people think. The idea of not having an answer to every question that could be asked is scary, as is dreaming a little bigger or differently to others. Most companies feel like they need people who are professionals who can defend everything, who have thought through every single scenario.

We need people to embrace messiness, to accept that real progress comes from things that are never done perfectly the first time. Young companies talk about the idea of a minimal viable product (MVP) which are ideas developed enough to see if there is something worth exploring further. Today we have processes like rapid prototyping or design sprints, or other ways to conceive, develop and test proposals far, far faster than a culture of perfection would ever allow.

Arguably, the innovation process in China is by nature faster and bolder thanks to its spirit of *chabuduo* which means 'it'll do' and *meibanfa*, aka 'can't be helped'. On the one hand it means things are never done perfectly, but on the other it allows rapid progress. Unlike in the West, people don't freak out if something doesn't work perfectly. China has a higher acceptance of imperfection, and that's reassuring if you are trying things that may totally mess up!

Maximize outcomes, don't minimize risk

Increasingly I feel that what drives a lot of work and roles is plausible deniability: it's less about making a difference and more about showing you did the right thing, even if it messed up. I know someone who works in A&R (artists and repertoire) for a record label (yes, still!) and whose role used to be very creative. It was about feeling and smelling which artists would break. They would listen to kids in playgrounds, go on online forums, sneak into gigs, go to sneaker stores, stalk people on Facebook. It was very emotionally driven and they were amazing at it. Now they've been asked to do it differently. They run programs that analyse sentiment online, they track trend lines and look at modelling, they scan social network size and clout. They now present the findings in meetings as data. They have never been less successful but they feel safer in their jobs than ever before. As Rory Sutherland says, 'It's much easier to be fired for being illogical than being unimaginative' (Sutherland, 2017). We have to change this. If you succeed thanks to a reckless emotional outpouring people think you were lucky; if you do something based on data and it screws up, people feel far less vulnerable. We have to create cultures that love oddness.

We need to get way better at being comfortable with being uncomfortable, with hating consensus and loving chaos and energy.

A sensible view on data

My (true) story that kicked off this chapter is a powerful example of the danger of data. Data can only reflect the reality of today, which is a terrible problem in a world that appears to change faster than ever and best rewards those who are first to new things.

A disease of the modern age is the need to support arguments with data. If we only ever built bridges where we could see people swimming across rivers, we would have not built many. We live for data-driven insights and I've never seen one. Data-supported arguments are fine but these days we don't treat data with enough scorn.

We need to have a more disdainful attitude towards most of the data that we see. Most data about the future is based on the linear interpolations of incorrect questions. If you ask people about that propensity to buy something that doesn't yet exist, you get something worse than useless – you get something damagingly misleading.

Create a process to change

Steps to transformation

I've seen a lot of documents outlining a magical number of steps to 'transformation'. They are all rooted in research and smart thinking, I'm just not that sure we've got time. When something new arrives in the world, we set up specialist units to deal with it. We cordon off a part of the building or set up an office in Austin. We buy funkier and brighter sofas, employ people who are younger and wear more casual clothes and we buy neon signage, all to deal with the new thing. First it was interactive, then it was mobile, then social, then maybe a content wing or chatbot practice.

We employ people to lead this charge, we get a chief innovation officer (gulp), or a head of digital strategy, we employ people to drive this change. As these units take root we fund them. We set up innovation labs. We buy 3D printers and a drone and stick them in a room with a robot vacuum and a VR headset. Trust me. We get experts in to come and speak. It's easy to do it this way. Innovation is compartmentalized and sanitized and merchandised. But it's not the way to effect change.

The more you are 'outside' the company, the easier it is to look vital, to evangelize, to be funky and to signpost to the outside world that the company is taking innovation and disruption and technology and change seriously. But the harder it is to actually get stuff done. To bring about change you need to be in meetings, you need to understand the problems faced, the reality of how things get done. You need to have authority to be a total pain and to challenge. To barge into meetings. It's less about a 5,000-cell spreadsheet showing interesting start-ups; it's more about playing golf with the CEO, infiltrating a private dinner, barging into a key meeting uninvited. Change is tough.

So while I believe in the 'many steps' theory, I think the ultimate goal of heads of innovation is the same as a head of digital in 2010 or a head of computerization in 1995 or a head of electricity in 1940: it's to make themselves redundant. To create a culture of innovation in everyone. The first step in that journey is to show everyone your intentions, to employ such a figurehead, but with the clear goal of moving out of the way and behind everyone.

We see lots of companies really failing to make alterations at a deep enough level. They tend to give up. For example, many banks or insurance companies will create a digital bank subsidiary. It's clearly the easiest step to undertake because it's moving everything messy to one side, but it's the integration that's hard – the politics, the interfaces between data on old systems and new.

The other approach often seen is building a newer digital facade onto the old structure and company. We see airlines with amazing snazzy new mobile apps, that look very slick, but won't allow you to change flights because that relies on the back end to be rebuilt.

Work like a start-up, but mean it

With the culture in place, and a process for change in place, how hard can this be? Well, now you have to get people working like you.

I've worked with a few large clients over the years, and while they loved the idea of working like a start-up, it was a bit like wanting to go to Glastonbury, but only if you got to avoid everything about a large music festival. The allure of working like start-ups, but in a sort of polite, 9–5, big corporate backing kind of way. They wanted to work like a start-up, but had $100 million to spend. They wanted to be agile and nimble, but with a complex approval process. We want to challenge everything, but with the data to support it. Let's go crazy, but please use existing marketing partners, let's break new ground but 'our competitors haven't done it yet'.

'We're going to act like a start-up' is a new corporate mantra. What would the founders of Klarna do here? How would Spotify market this? How can we replicate WeWork's approach? Yet it never works that way. Spreadsheets need to be filled in showing target user numbers, someone back-fills profitability requirements, someone calculates projected revenue, and automatically an investment level is found.

All with no idea that this is all the antithesis of start-ups. Start-ups hustle, they ask favours, and they use the limitation of money to force themselves to try risky things.

The role of IT

Most corporate IT systems are relatively complicated, and they know that the CEO is unlikely ever to question it. We have roles like the chief information officer (CIO), who never wants the headache of really investigating a new system, when the old one will just about do. Rather like the idea that no one ever gets fired for buying an IBM, no one ever gets promoted for doing something that takes time, money, and doesn't really need to be done yet. But as we saw at the end of 2017, with a computer glitch that allowed all American Airlines' pilots to take time off over the Christmas holiday, the role of IT is incredibly central to what needs to be done, yet budgets are near impossible to get. CTOs now have budgets that are divided between keeping the show on the road, and providing functionality. Legacy system upgrades can only be achieved at the expense of investments in newer systems elsewhere. As a result, what happens is like all innovation: it's the front-end systems that are favoured. While it makes sense that the customer's system is shiny and new and built by the best teams with the best software, the reality is that most people's experience is somewhat reliant on the more boring, less visible systems behind this. Those needing quick fixes for archaic sites use tools like XML-based web services, middle-wear technology, and portal frameworks that enable them to prolong the life of the fundamental operating systems that underpin many of the early 1980s systems.

The role of IT has always been seen as a support function. Rather like the human resource department, it is behind the scenes and noticed only when it doesn't do things well. We need to think of it in a different way: less as a support function and more as an investment vehicle for leading a path through change. IT should be one of the most vital departments of any company. It should be full of people excited about the future, investigating the latest software to do their expenses, enthusiastically testing new timesheet programs, or better ways to manage invoices. Many companies are let down by legacy systems that, even though they work, take up a lot of time.

Hack legislation

There is an incredible relationship between regulation and rules, and innovation.

Companies have often referred to the Fosbury Flop as a way to show what happens when people think differently. Over the years, various athletes had been setting high-jump records with the strad-dle jump, or the barrel roll. By 1978 the bar had been set so high and improvements had become so slight, that the record appeared unlikely to change much at 2.34m (7ft 8in).

The story is that Dick Fosbury dared to think differently, reached much greater heights and created a world record by going over the high-jump bar backwards. Something that is never really mentioned in this story is the role of rules, and the technology involved. It was only because mattresses had been allowed to get thicker that the entire notion of the backwards jump suddenly made sense. In fact, many people had been very keen to jump this way for years, but they just knew it would probably injure them.

Lyft first broke taxi regulations by asking for donations, not demanding payment. Airbnb basically lives on the edge of the law at all times. Many new innovations can thrive at the edge of legality. Vaping is entirely disruptive because nobody knows what laws to regulate with, drones live in a weird area with poor legislation, intellectual property law is woefully behind the times.

What new businesses need to do about this is understand that regulation and the legal system will always be behind the pace of technology and society's development. Companies can understand the implications of this, and either seek to maximize what they can gain in the grey space, or at least quickly realize the degree to which they can stick to the spirit and not the letter of the law.

What do insurgents wish they had?

At this moment in time it's very easy to be overwhelmed at the success of the Amazons and the Facebooks of the world. It's very easy to look at the way they have been able to grow, and feel pessimistic about your opportunities. It's easy to think that life is unfair, and they have all the benefits.

The reality is that most existing companies have many assets that they take for granted. If you're a retailer, having a physical premise on every High Street or Main Street is obviously costly, and feels like a disadvantage. But at the same time it offers incredible advantages, whether it's the amount of trust that it creates, the ability to provide immediate delivery, or the ability to upsell people at the point of purchase. Companies like banks need to realize that their very physical manifestation endows them with extraordinary trust with the members of the public. Through their staff, they have built long-term and significant relationships with their customers.

So it is imperative that companies today consider things from other companies' perspectives. They need to map out 'What does Amazon wish that they had?' and explore, and exploit, that gap. They need to think 'What do car makers with hundreds of years of experience wish they had?' Maybe it's a dealership network. Maybe it's a long history of knowing how quickly the prices of their vehicles will depreciate with age. Every company needs to seek out what their competitors wish they had and really focus on that point of difference.

Leverage the power of expert generalists

Francis Crick and James Watson were not particularly well-regarded scientists. They had shown no more promise than others. What they had was something that nobody else did: a width of expertise across different fields. As pretty much the only people alive who had knowledge of X-ray diffraction, chemistry and biological expertise, they had skills in all the required areas to enable them to join the dots and discover the structure of DNA.

We tend to fall in love with the idea of the expert. We tend to assume that new technology needs a deep expertise. We think that everything that arrives is more complicated than we can imagine, and that we need to place our trust in people who understand everything about these technologies and these changes. Increasingly, the real success comes from building different bridges between different lines of thoughts – by connecting dots between two different disciplines. While it's always going to be important to have specialists, industry probably needs to celebrate more the people who can span these different areas, apply creative thought, learn from one area and apply it to another.

I suffer from back pain a lot. I know of no doctor who knows enough about it all to know who I should best seek treatment from. Instead I have to meet chiropractors, physiotherapists, neurosurgeons, orthopaedic spine surgeons; each will claim the solution they have to offer is just what is needed.

Car companies now need people who understand software design and how people drive. Retailers need people who understand browsing behaviour and how people behave at the point of sale. TV companies need to understand how to make great TV, but also how younger people's behaviours have changed and what streaming technology allows.

'When all you have is a hammer, every problem looks like a nail' is a very true saying. A key thing for businesses as they look forward to the future is to find ways to encourage curious people to think differently about problems, to apply creativity in new ways, and to challenge everyone to think differently.

Use imagination

We tend to only really understand new technology when viewed through the frame of the old. The very first TV shows were radio plays with cameras pointed at them. Websites today look pretty similar to digitalized forms of paper in the past. Our imagination is pretty weak. Even a creature like the unicorn, designed to represent something new, mythical, and outrageous, is still based on two existing animals combined.

No one ever predicted the internet before it existed. It was like nothing we had ever seen before, and nothing we could possibly imagine. No one ever really conceptualized the idea of cryptocurrencies, or decentralized banking systems, because those notions didn't exist, at all, before.

Companies need to get much better at thinking about the future, less in terms of combining existing elements, and more about creating things that have never existed before. This obviously places incredible demands on our imagination and the creative process, but it's essential for companies if they wish to get the benefit of ground-breaking thinking – that they are able to do something radically different to anything that's been done before.

Span software, hardware and services

Generally speaking in the world there are physical companies trying to get digital, and digitally led companies trying to embrace physical. 'Is Walmart going to get e-commerce before Amazon gets brick and mortar?' is the classic question, but we see the battle everywhere and it's a false dichotomy.

The jaw-droppingly expensive and beautiful Devialet speakers sound like they come from heaven, yet the app you use to control them is less impressive. When you buy the speakers you get access to exclusive live broadcast concerts and over their lifetime they update with greater connectivity and better sound quality.

Brands and businesses need to think less of what they make and more about how it feels in all senses. The experience of shopping online now includes the packaging, the bill you get from your utility company may be offset by how easy it is to pay, how much extra would it cost to make a Nespresso machine that auto orders coffee capsules and how much more money would that make? What would happen if a TV maker felt the menu design and the remote control were important to make beautiful, what if they came with exclusive apps? More than anything else we need to think in terms of long-term relationships, how do we keep car buyers coming back to the brand, how can we ensure we go from a Samsung TV to a Samsung smart home?

By thinking of the physical and virtual, access not ownership, holistic not device, we can increase the power of what we offer and our ability to charge a premium.

Be drastic, not agile

'Move fast and break things', 'Test and learn', 'Dynamic optimization', 'Fail fast', we've all embraced the thinking of the modern age and this always-on and agile approach. Clearly moving fast is good, clearly bureaucracy is bad, but sometimes I'm not sure we think. Often corporate strategy for large firms seems to be missing. There isn't a bold vision, progress is an algorithm, we A–B test ourselves to the future. This isn't inherently bad, but it reduces the chance of bold progress. Most companies today are typically just trying to keep up with the needs of today, they are merely trying to work hard to stay the same distance behind.

If we think of companies as skyscrapers (see Chapter 1), or as a mainline railway line that's old and crumbling, one reaches a point where it's better to rebuild than it is to maintain. Software gets bloated and unknown, people get jaded and bitter, organizational charts groan under the weight, hardware becomes out of date.

I wonder sometimes if we need the opposite to agile. We need sudden leaps forward and then periods of stability. We need systems and processes designed in tandem with each other. We need to leap to create brand new entities based on the latest thinking and software, and periods of calm where we change little. It's a bold new way to think about change, it's countercultural, but it's interesting to ponder.

Be optimistic

There are incredible opportunities for companies who get this right. Each and every one of these ways of thinking is positive in nature, but taken together, they can feel overwhelming. Press coverage and general discussions in business today tend to focus on the negative only. We continually focus on the companies that got it wrong or that didn't change. It's very difficult for people to feel overly optimistic.

As you walk around the world today, you see signs of this. You see very, very few companies enthusiastically embracing what they could be doing. I would love to see old companies change their approach. The day that computer-aided design entered architecture practices saw the launch of a plethora of new forms, and ideals, and ideas being developed. Frank Gehry or Santiago Calatrava did not have to change in order to stay in business; they did so because they felt incredibly excited to do things that had never been done before.

References

Atkins, R and Bradshaw, T (2017) Nestlé breaks into US hipster coffee market with Blue Bottle deal, *Financial Times*, 14 September, available from: https://www.ft.com/content/8fccb91a-9943-11e7-a652-cde3f882dd7b [last accessed 7 December 2017]

Bariso, J (2017) This e-mail from Elon Musk to Tesla employees describes what great communication looks like, INC, 30 August, available from: https://www.inc.com/justin-bariso/this-email-from-elon-musk-to-tesla-employees-descr.html [last accessed 7 December 2017]

Haldane, A (2010) Patience and Finance [online], 2 September, available from: https://www.bankofengland.co.uk/-/media/boe/files/speech/2010/patience-and-finance-speech-by-andrew-haldane.pdf [last accessed 7 December 2017]

Keller, S and Meaney, M (2017) Attracting and retaining the right talent, McKinsey and Company, available from: https://www.mckinsey.com/business-functions/organization/our-insights/attracting-and-retaining-the-right-talent [last accessed 7 December 2017]

Millman, D (1980) *The Way of the Peaceful Warrior: A book that changes lives*, H J Kramer, CA

Molla, R (2017) Tech companies spend more on R&D than any other companies in the US, *Recode*, 1 September, available from: https://www.recode.net/2017/9/1/16236506/tech-amazon-apple-gdp-spending-productivity [last accessed 7 December 2017]

Primack, D (2016) Unilever buys Dollar Shave Club for $1billion, *Fortune*, 20 July, available from: http://fortune.com/2016/07/19/unilever-buys-dollar-shave-club-for-1-billion/ [last accessed 7 December 2017]

Sacks, D (2014) The multimillion dollar quest to brew the perfect cup of coffee, *Fast Company*, 18 August, available from: https://www.fastcompany.com/3033306/the-multimillion-dollar-quest-to-brew-the-perfect-cup-of-coffee [last accessed 7 December 2017]

Sutherland, R (2017) Mastering the Future of Marketing, speech at the dotmailer Summit, London, 1 March 2017

Weinmann, K and Groth, A (2011) The shortest-tenured CEOs in history, *Business Insider*, 23 September, available from: http://www.businessinsider.com/ceos-short-tenures-2011-9?IR=T [last accessed 7 December 2017]

Winsor, J (2017) The Hamptons Effect – What's stopping you from being innovative? [blog], LinkedIn Pulse, 13 January, available from: https://www.linkedin.com/pulse/hamptons-effect-whats-stopping-you-from-being-john-winsor/ [last accessed 7 December 2017]

YCharts (2017) Nestlé research and development expense (semi annual) [online] available from: https://ycharts.com/companies/NSRGY/r_and_d_expense_sa [last accessed 7 December 2017]

PART THREE
Anticipating the future

08
A changing canvas

People are funny. The top two things most people complain about are 'the way things are' and 'change in the world'. We need to get better at loving what is new, and establishing what to worry about and what to embrace, what to ignore and what to obsess over. This chapter is an attempt to do that.

It's hard in business and in life right now. What we need more than ever is simplicity, people to spend time joining the dots together, ignoring distractions, plotting a path through change and making the complex easier to understand.

This chapter will describe the clear movements over time that businesses can exploit *now*. These are demonstrable movements we see today and that we can work from. Unlike Chapters 9 and 10 that follow, this chapter is looking less into the future. It's not a guess of what could come, it's the here and now, and it's often misunderstood. These themes are more about connecting the dots we see today and around the world. These are themes that may appear to be somewhat futuristic in nature, but are merely a snapshot of some of the most contemporary things on this planet at this moment.

Digital disappointment

The greasy fingerprints told only half the tale. Large plasma screens littered the departure lounge, but despite (or possibly because of) their oversized font, the perfect height of the monitors, and the very slow refresh rate of data, affixed to each and every one was a peeling printed label: 'This is not a touchscreen.'

Digital disappointment surrounds us. Everything should be faster, more accurate, and personalized. Anything new progresses from magical, to wonderful, to expected, to disappointing in a matter of moments.

The only things that consistently move faster than technological advancements are our expectations of them. The lag delays further, the gap between what we expect and what we get grows larger, and delight fades quickly to disappointment. It's getting worse.

My phone can access everything ever made by anyone anywhere immediately – but why is this taking so long? When I can get 4G on the Shanghai underground, why can't I get reception in the elevator? Why can't I stream this abroad? But my other bank uses Touch ID. You don't have Uber here yet? Why can't you remember my username? And for all the promise of big data, my credit card provider is still sending monthly sign-up offers by post.

Surrounded by mismanaged expectations, the beat of modern life is disappointment.

Technology for many is something we only notice when it's not working. Toddlers look aghast that the TV isn't touch-enabled. Teens are exasperated that angry tweets are not replied to within minutes. And it's only spreading upward to older people, further away from the bleeding edge. As companies built for the modern age slowly replace their industrial incumbents, we now see each best-in-class experience as the standard for all.

As the process of technological disruption reaches maturity in some industries, it hasn't even begun in others. We're now left with the laggards: banks that refuse to see the future and insist on maintaining high-street locations rather than perfecting customer service; insurance companies that refuse to accept the changing world of Zipcar and Airbnb; healthcare systems based on paper; and immigration and tax policies yet to accept that planes and the internet exist or that jobs can be freelanced.

What can companies do about digital disappointment?

Chapter 11 of this book will focus on customer experience in the new world, and will discuss the need for empathy and technology, but for now just take on this realization that companies need to get better at understanding life from a customer's perspective. Companies think that customers compare the booking flow of their mobile operator with that of other mobile operators, when they actually compare it with any form they have ever typed information into.

Companies need to look around and further afield

Every company needs to consider the competitor and comparison set of every single experience a customer may have, not just those in their category. Experience isn't limited by anything. Luxury retailers look at other luxury retailers, but never further afield. Banks benchmark against other banks. Airlines do the same. We need to get better at considering every single amazing experience we have as stimulus for ideation. If a hotel in Dubai googles you and establishes it's your birthday, why can't your airline? If you can buy things in one click on Amazon, why not on a banking website? We need to look at best-in-class solutions from anywhere. These best-in-class solutions are likely to be found around the world in a variety of places. Often we can learn the most by looking at luxury brands, or companies in Asia, but especially by looking at new companies who've employed the best and latest technology.

Business must do the basics well first

Chains are as strong as their weakest link. Companies need to get much better at shoring up the worst part of the experience, doing all basic things right, before having a strong platform to perform the extravagant extras. It is hard because you don't get famous this way. The fact that Verizon always works for me, that Chase's website is never down, that Delta Air Lines' staff are always just lovely, that Quartz is just a beautiful, well-designed news site with great articles is rarely celebrated. But that doesn't mean I don't notice their competitors that fail.

Time limited, stuff abundant

Growing up in a small Cotswold village in the middle of England in the 1980s, I remember boredom. When the TV station Channel 5 launched in the UK, we were propelled into a future with 25 per cent more stuff to do; the maths was that easy. Even with five TV channels, my Dad's trusty VHS recorder, and access to the village shop video rental library, I remember being bored. I remember watching snooker or lawn bowls on TV, or the *Antiques Roadshow*. I remember listening to the chart show on the radio, fingers poised over 'record' and 'play' buttons, patiently and avidly waiting for the songs I liked to come on to be recorded. A lot of my youth was about being both bored and focused, paying full attention to things I didn't really like, I guess making the most of scarcity.

It dawns on me now that I've not been bored since about 2004. Our primary challenge today is operating in an environment where we cram 31 hours and 28 minutes of activity into every 24-hour day. To do this we multitask, we shop as we check our phones, have the radio on while we cook, we have tablets on laps, phones in hand, TV on in the background. An abundance of stuff is now created, social posts, photos from friends, more scripted TV shows than ever before. More movies, more songs, more websites, more of everything. We have far too much stuff, and far too little time.

Often trends appear to work like Newtonian physics: for every action there is an equal and opposite reaction. It's the uniform reliability of a Bud Light that makes the craft beer movement make sense, it's the boring but comfy assurance of Holiday Inn Expresses that make the 'will-they-really-be-there-when-I-get-there?' fun of Airbnb work. Consumerism is the same. Those who grew up under communism and pretend-equality now seek a way to express themselves and their status with an enduring love of luxury brands. It is the bland sameness of brutalist apartments in Bucharest that mean a thriving culture of interior design and some of the most eye-bleedingly expensive interior design stores I've ever seen.

It is this same dynamic that explains a shift away from stuff in most of the Western world. Those 30-year-olds growing up today in the developed world probably had a childhood of rampant consumerism and more than enough stuff. If you got the TV you wanted when you were 15, got clothing for bargain prices at 16, then you've never really known scarcity. But then suddenly you don't love the idea of stuff.

It is now clear in this era that our big problem in life isn't scarcity; it's abundance, and in every way. We have too many careers we could have had, too many cities we could have lived in, too many people we could have married, too many restaurants we could have eaten at. And when you understand this, you are better able to forge a company fit for these people.

Steps to work in the age of abundance

Three things are apparent from this shift to a world of too much stuff and too little time.

1. Make it easier for people to buy your products

Everything you sell should be as simple as possible. Casper offers one mattress, Allbirds one type of shoe. We have long worked on the idea of the 'long tail', that someone will buy everything one day. Increasingly we either need to offer a very small number of items for sale, or use personalization software to appear that way, to be unique for everyone. And let's shorten the purchase funnel, let's make advertising shoppable. Our phones, tablets, laptops, watches and increasingly TVs are now the storefront for every retailer in the world. Our devices now know our credit card details, or shipping address, and should soon know our sizes, tastes and needs. In theory every ad on the internet could be shippable with a swipe of the finger or press of the thumb or shout out to Alexa.

2. Make it easier to extract more money from people

Some industries have grown up with a long history and track record of getting way more money out of people in a simple way. Airlines charge for speedy boarding and seat selection in the booking process but in a booking flow that is so seamless that it never felt like it got in the way. Physical retailers offer small impulse purchases in the lines to pay. But this thinking isn't everywhere.

People are busy, they don't have time to think; the mental burden, the cost of time taken, are often more expensive than spending money. Separate people from money faster than ever before.

3. Make products that stand out and create demand

There is this weird sense that somehow the importance of branding is dying, alongside advertising. Nothing could be further from the truth. The more choices we face in life, the less it appears we want to buy things; the less time we have, the more vital clear branding and sense of meaning become. Of course, it's trite to say 'make better things'. We know that already. Every person in every business should be thinking how to make a meaningfully better kettle, pair of jeans, training shoe… . I think there is massive potential for companies to succeed with simply great products. But there is also potential in making brands that just connect more strongly.

We can go from being receptive to the idea of buying something to wanting a specific product now, immediately. The two best examples of this are the iPhone and the Tesla 3.

Before the iPhone, people were largely sold phones or were given them for free. You re-signed your contract and saw what you could get as a reward. People took little interest in phones. The decision architecture was, 'Do I need to re-sign my contract?', 'Which operator should I pick and then what tariff?'. In 2002 you'd select from a flip phone or a candy-bar phone or in 2004 you'd pick a camera phone or a music phone or an 'enterprise' phone for e-mail. In 2007, the iPhone entirely changed the purchase funnel. People went from being 'sold to' to 'buying', from choosing a phone based on network to choosing a network based on phone, from waiting until the contract ends to 'I don't care how much I'll be fined for ending it now'.

The Tesla 3 is somewhat the same. People replace cars when leases are up; they decide what sort of car, then narrow down brands, then test drive a few and make a choice. The Tesla 3 has got people with new cars wanting to switch, people with different formats of cars wanting to change car type. I have no need for a car: I hate owning things, parking costs a fortune, and while I have no desire to buy a car, I kind of want to have a Tesla 3. It's this sort of allure and product differentiation and brand that companies must aspire to own.

Pervasive internet

If you ask a typical 60-year-old how much time they spend online, they may say three hours per day; ask a similarly representative 40-year-old and they may say they use the internet for four hours a day. Generally speaking younger people spend more time per day online. A 20-year-old may say they spend five hours per day online. Yet if you ask a 14-year-old, and trust me I have, many times, they go quiet. They can't answer the question. The youth of today don't have an 'online' because the concept of 'offline' doesn't exist. Remember when we typed into chatrooms the letters BRB (be right back)? The youth of today don't do this because they never leave.

Consuming is just part of being alive; it's not a behaviour, it just is. We misunderstand the world around us because of our memories and the way we've slowly added things to adapt to the new world. My first experiences of the internet came around 1997 at university. I remember hearing about e-mail, being given an account and much like the first person on the planet with a telephone, wondering just who it was that I could write to. It was a long time before I could get my parents to get an e-mail account or even the internet. What would it do? We've been fine until now. E-mail was confusing and new, and even now they share an e-mail account, because that's what addresses are: the place you both check mail.

Have you noticed today how rarely we see on/off buttons? Most devices like TVs, phones, tablets, sound docks, are things in a permanent state of quasi on. The internet is the same. We now have the notion of ambient connectivity. We've always assumed connected things had screens, modems 'went' online; increasingly, if things have power, it's almost always the case that they have potential to be connected. From lightbulbs to art frames, toasters to cars, house keys to phones, TVs to clocks, speakers to thermostats, the world is one of connected devices. We're moving from items to systems; it's less about the individual item and more about the holistic ecosystem. What increasingly will make things special is how they work with others and how they create solutions rather than do things. The smart home is a long way off, but when it comes together, works seamlessly around us, it will bring about a profound shift: thermostats that talk to automatic blinds to keep apartments cool and save energy, lighting that knows where you are, turns off and on as you leave, and changes colour and mood based on the time of day and your calendar.

What can companies do about it?

1. Change our mental model

We have constructed and adapted companies as the internet has developed by adding things on. When the internet first arrived, we bolted on 'interactive' departments and then relabelled them 'digital' departments. We found new people who understood the technology best, created small teams, kept them at arm's length and invited them to some meetings. As the world evolved we repeated the same process, getting 'social' departments, then 'mobile' departments, each with their own area to work in, P&L and clients or agencies to serve or be served. We built a structure that still insists on seeing the world from our memories. We still talk about e-commerce or m-commerce when it's just how people buy things in the modern world. We didn't call catalogue shopping 'phone' commerce; how things get to people isn't interesting. We talk about streaming TV vs linear TV, a distinction that means nothing to people. We label some channels social media, when pretty much all media is now social and all social media is essentially just media to people.

People today do not do 'e-banking'; they pay people, scan cheques, make deposits, regardless of the pipes used to convey information. They don't do digital photography, or online dating, or buy e-tickets to events; they take pictures, date people and see shows. Spotify is different to radio in that you can control what you get, not because it comes to you via a different infrastructure.

We have to entirely change our mindset, work around people and not channels, explore better ways to serve people and take their money in return, find better ways to make advertising that flows across screens and contexts and not focus on how things get to them. As discussed earlier, our companies need to be structurally aligned around people, not delivery technologies.

2. Form bridges

We talk a lot about 'online' as if it's still 2005. People today don't go online. We don't plug in modems or dial up. We don't spend time surfing the web, e-banking or online dating. Being online is just life in 2017. We continue to keep trying to segment life as digital or non-digital. We talk about 'digital influencing' and 'mobile influencing' 56 per cent and 37 per cent of purchase decisions, respectively (Marketing Charts, 2016). When we do so, it shows we have no clue about people today.

Our reality isn't augmented with headsets; it's augmented with information. Our phones serve as the primary conduit, but the additions of the Amazon Dash button, Google Home speaker, tablet or laptop and others have created a truly hybrid world. The next stage is to better bridge reality with the lattice of the internet. For example, while I'm not quite as excited about voice as many are, TV ads that instruct you to ask Alexa to order something are interesting and reduce complexity. As Alexa, Siri, Bixby are built into phones and devices, you'll soon be able to speak and get help anywhere.

Geolocation is another example. In theory, your phone could show train times as you wait on the platform. Your gym app could open as you walk into its lobby. Airlines could check you in as you get to the terminal. When the real world and online are connected by where we are, we can automatically be served relevant information and outputs.

QR codes could be the solution

QR codes have dominated life in Japan since the late 1990s, and have since taken off in China, but have never really been adopted in the West (Loras, 2015). Nobody understood what they were or what to do with them. They required a special app to be downloaded or had to be embedded in another app. The mixture of no clear use cases, no existing behaviour, and friction to download has killed any attempts. I actually tried making the West's first QR code ad campaign in 2005, but I think they were only scanned twice (and that may have been by me).

QR codes have many advantages. They are free to use, free to make and free to distribute – it's just an image that can be created dynamically in seconds. They can be featured anywhere you want: in magazines and stores, on clothing and signs. They can be encrypted, secure, and thus used for payments. By their very nature, QR codes create a virtuous circle in reverse.

Spotify now embeds QR-style codes in their app so that you can share music in seconds, and Shazam uses them to make business cards come to life in AR. More recently, Apple has embedded automatic scanning of QR codes in the iOS camera function, and Google added them as a clear option on Chrome. We now have over one billion devices that can access them.

If we can now find a way to leverage QR codes to make great experiences and reward people, the future could present fascinating opportunities for delivering real value to consumers and real ROI to brands across the customer journey. We could automatically convert awareness and consideration to purchase by creating print ads from which you can buy products directly. We could scan spirit bottles to see cocktail recipes with links to additional ingredients, and reorder a pair of jeans we love by merely snapping a picture of their label, thus driving additional purchase and retention.

QR codes represent a vastly under-tapped technology when it comes to delivering true value to consumers across their journey, and missed opportunities for brands to create two of the most critical contributors to purchases: loyalty and advocacy; and increased touchpoints and reduced friction. When we look at what the consumer actually needs from technology like QR codes, we'll deliver so much more for them and for brands.

Create experiences that flow across devices

Digital convergence now means that most devices are rather similar in nature. We once had single-purpose devices that did very different things. Radios, TVs, Walkmans, video players, answerphones. Things were all different, and each was a key part of an ecosystem: TVs and TV remote controls with TV shows and TV transmitters and TV channels.

Now devices are functionally very similar. Tablets are ostensibly big phones. Laptops are bigger tablets with keyboards. Smart TVs are bigger tablets but without touchscreens, even smartwatches have more in common with a tablet than a watch. Most of our commonly used items are essentially (pardon the expression) black mirrors: rectangular glass monoliths that display moving images, are connected to the internet, offer sound, and connect to each other with technology like Bluetooth. What's fascinating about these separate items is not what they do, but the context used for their consumption. Tablets and laptops to some extent are primarily work-based devices to input data and get stuff done. TVs become lean-back screens, to let us sit more passively and be entertained. Smartphones become key glanceable surfaces to see micro-nuggets of information, but also (as yet mainly untapped) a way to interact with the real world, either as a payment band, a way to unlock hotel or home doors or even cars, or to act as boarding passes for planes, entry devices for secure offices, tickets for events. Our phone is increasingly not just the primary way that we interact with others, or acquire information, but increasingly serves as the entry point to other screens. It is the sun of our digital solar system.

Intimate screens and data

I'm not sure when data got big. Something must have happened a few years ago when we were not watching, or at night, when we passed an arbitrary marker of size. When we say 'big data', it appears we just mean more of it. We now have more sensors, measuring more things, and with more connectivity we can share it more readily. Greater processing power and cheaper storage means we can do more with it. Sounds great, but so what?

It's my opinion that the main power of data lies in informing and making decisions, and then evaluating the decisions we've made. Literally, that's all data is for. When we talk about the size of data we celebrate the wrong thing. What we really need is the ability to make better decisions, faster and about more important things, and then optimize based on this. Big data is really about profound decision-making. In this context we can see that what really matters is the data's robustness, its cleanliness, and its intimacy, not its size. Fortunately, changing consumption patterns are making this easier.

The primary screens in our lives have changed over time. The first screen in our lives, in the late 1800s, was the cinema. A massive screen that we watched with many other people, that we sat far away from, and over which we had little control. We could either be in the movie theatre or walk out. The next screen invented was the TV screen, nearly 100 years later, and here we gathered closer to a smaller screen with fewer people, but we had more control, we could change channels and volume. Computers, both laptops and PCs, came next, a smaller screen to which we got a lot closer, and shared with only one or two others. On this screen we could go anywhere, we had the internet at our disposal, the most control we'd ever known.

So far, the latest and newest screen in our life has been the smartphone. We see the exact same trend lines. It's the smallest screen we've ever known, it's the one that we watch from the shortest distance, typically a few inches away. It's the one that we are most in control of. We can touch it, tap it, shake it, press harder and it will allow a much more tactile and immersive experience, but above all else it's the most personal. This means at any moment in time your screen knows where you are, what you are likely to do, how you are feeling, who you know. It knows the weather, the time of day, your mood, your likes, recent searches; this device knows more about you than perhaps you do.

When a TV repair person comes around our house we don't mind leaving them alone. When our work computers are being updated, we're a little more worried. Phones are different. Get a person to unlock their phone and pass to someone else for a few seconds and tension appears immediately. Phones are the most personal things we've ever known. Between the stress levels that can be detected in our voice, our activity levels from accelerometers, locations visited, barometric pressure recordings, social activity, browsing behaviour, our phones know everything about us. They can reasonably figure out the weather where we are, where we plan on being, what we've done, and to some degree what we're thinking and need.

In theory this trend should continue. We should have access to another smaller screen, one closer to us, measuring more intimate detail than anything else, more expansive and tactile in the experiences it can rely. It's this theory that suggests that smartwatches or VR headsets will become the norm. For me it's a big question about humanity. We have, without exception, hated technology on our face; from Google Glass to Snap Spectacles, our faces are too vital to be augmented until society moves on. I can see VR not as the next smartphone or the next TV set, but as a large niche within gaming, but nothing more. Smartwatches have a greater chance of success, but I can't see them being fashionable. The real estate on many people is there to express who you are, not to suggest that you're obsessed with your body's metrics or that you need to know everything now. To some extent being disconnected, being demonstrably in the moment, will probably soon become the ultimate in status.

Use the power of intimate data

The first change comes from data. If we're wearing watches, clever clothes and using sentient spoons, our heartbeat, moods, location, stress levels, calendars and search activity are all being recorded, shared and analysed. If we circumvent for now the obvious privacy concerns, we're armed with the best data we've ever had. Forget big data. When you have intimate data, little else seems important.

Target people at moments

The ads of the future may be promoted routes in our cars, notifications on our smartphones that it's about to rain and an Uber is close, or money-off codes for holiday resorts when sensors on our smartphones detect we're getting stressed.

Personalize communications

There is no time in my life when I am less likely to buy some white trousers, a toaster or a flight to Los Angeles than after I've just bought these items, yet that's precisely the time I see ads for these products or services.

We can do better than this when more and more behavioural data is overlaid with checkout data, credit card data and recommendation engines. We will soon see a new era of personalized advertising. We'll be shown ads for big-ticket items at precisely the right time, after we've been thinking about them for a predetermined period. We'll be shown ads for items that work perfectly with our new white trousers. Technology is moving so fast that soon both the ad placement and the advertisement itself will become automated.

We'll see fully-rendered completely personalized video ads based on real-time pricing, real-time availability, the weather and thousands of other data points. The art director and copywriter team of the future is the algorithm and processor.

One-on-one communications with instant messaging

The fastest growing technology and behaviour the world has ever seen has been the incredible rise of instant messaging (IM). Its rapid growth has destroyed the text message business and put the power of instant, peer-to-peer communication in the hands of over 2.5 billion people around the world, though this is expected to grow to 3.6 billion by 2018 (*The Economist*, 2016). Yet few if any businesses or ad agencies seem to have noticed.

The scant marketing conversation going on seems to entirely miss the point. Most companies see sponsored emojis or branded keyboards as the way to explore this world. Even less imagination seems to have been used by the myriad of companies hoping to inject advertising into our most personal conversations. In fact, this channel represents a whole new way to think about retail, customer service and how we experience brands and the notion of one-on-one customer relationship management. Collectively the advertising world spends around $600 billion per year putting messages out there. We hope that with all of this wondrous messaging and smart targeting people will click or buy or call up or find out more. The hope is that 'people want conversations with brands,' yet businesses often refuse to offer e-mail customer services, let alone IM.

A generation of people have grown up hating phone calls. Even those that grew up with them now prefer any form of brief written communication over verbal. In fact 72 per cent of people (according to a TeleTech study) think phone calls are the worst way to undertake customer service.

There are several key unique advantages of IM over phone calls and e-mails:

- *Secure*: unlike e-mail, snail mail or even phone calls, IMs can be a guaranteed way to reach the specific, correct, single person. Using Touch ID, cameras or facial recognition to unlock phones creates the most secure platform we've even known. No more pin numbers or passwords; just frictionless personal, secure service.

- *Asynchronous and immediate*: nobody likes waiting for call backs or for slow computers. IM offers both immediate and asynchronous communication, which allows multitasking while the customer services representative investigates. It also stops dropped signal areas from interrupting calls and means customer services can work with several people at the same time.

- *More informative*: IM platforms allow messages to include location maps, images, videos, money, attachments and other rich items, which allow a far better conversational exchange. Want to see what shoes are left in stock? A quick IM makes it possible.

What does this mean for business?

1. An opportunity for everyone

All service companies should be offering customer service and information via IM. There are no excuses for this not being text enabled. From ordering dry-cleaning collections to booking haircuts and buying items from designers directly or even getting the news, our primary mode of transactions on mobile could be within IM. Just imagine the possibilities.

Location-based technology allows people to order a pizza for delivery to their current location. Technology such as application programming interfaces (APIs) allow messaging to become embedded with other overlaying services. For example, Facebook Messenger allows people to order taxis from Uber, book restaurant tables using OpenTable, or nearby cinema seats from the Fandango API, quickly and securely.

Many airlines now offer remarkably good service over Twitter. You can now easily use it to change seats or rebook flights or cancel tickets, but why use the clumsy interface of Twitter when IM is faster, more secure and personal? From renting cars, to seeing where the rental car is, to checking the bill, to submitting receipts for expenses, IM will be the best platform for everything.

2. Don't conflate bots with IM

Chatbots are where two incredible and transformative technologies overlap: IM meets AI.

They are based on the concept and thinking of IM, and are powered by the engineering of AI. But the truth is they are not that good. The current state of AI, outside of the powerhouses of Google, Facebook, university labs and a handful of others, is most likely to be an advanced algorithm. In fact, the chatbot interfaces of today seem like a visualized user flow from a call-centre menu. Instead of 'press 1 for Spanish' and then '5 for customer service' we most often see limited menus pre-set to fixed questions, that we can't even try to bypass without causing issues. Type in anything close to a sensible sentence that hasn't been pre-set, and you quickly go into error territory.

For sales, generating leads or converting interest, chatbots seem to be an especially poor solution. To spend hundreds of millions in advertising dollars in the hope that in one magical moment a potential customer makes the effort to contact you, and to then in this moment of wonder pass them to a computer because you can't expend the power and cost of human interaction, seems particularly strange.

For customer service, when seen in this cost-savings context, the benefits of chatbots are more obvious to companies – transforming FAQ sections on websites into conversations, directing customer service questions to the best department, checking rates and opening times or updates on train routes or flights – the list of potential applications goes on.

Bifurcation of retail

Shopping is seeing the same split, moving from shopping as a 'branded experience' to buying as the 'ultimate in ease'.

Buying is simplicity

I'm pretty sure no person in modern times has ever been so bored that they went window shopping on Amazon; the spartan CMS, the ugly product shots and the functional taxonomy have all been designed to make buying as easy and seamless as possible. But never fun.

Shopping on Amazon, when it works best, isn't an experience; it's a lack of experience. It's unmemorable. I have bought books twice because I seemingly bought the first one in my sleep. It's the purest example yet of the act of removing every possible barrier, every piece of friction. The end result of countless A–B tests to optimize for simplicity, speed and efficiency.

This is the world of buying. It's the surgical operation of a system to reduce cognitive burden, to make decisions fast, facile and friction-less, if not automatic. The system was designed originally for people who know what they want and want to get what they need without thinking, yet it's become the default way to acquire goods in the age of too much choice and too little time.

So increasingly the world of retail seems to work this way. We have product reviews spreading across retail with quick-to-glance stars to give us confidence. We have the Wi-Fi-connected Amazon Dash button, which allows us to procure items with a nonchalant poke.

Shopping is experiential

Even the most ardent M&M's fan doesn't believe the 25,000 sq ft of M&M's World in Times Square, New York is there to satiate the cravings of New Yorkers for chocolate at 11:45 pm. Like all flagship stores M&M's World is there to impart an experience. It's shopping to be remembered, it's a journey of discovery, it's memorable, it's there to take time and savour. It's the opposite of buying.

Shopping is most often found in physical retail because it's the easiest to do with sights and smells. Shopping is the world of adding experiences. It's the interactive perfume lab in Selfridges, the selfie opportunities in Harvey Nichols, the Hardware Club experiences in Harrods or the extravagant fragrance laboratories of Le Labo. Coffee shops seem to have learned this: unnecessarily long wait, the drama of the brew, the theatre of the leather-bound menu in Intelligentsia Coffee.

Buying is what drives farmers' markets and their stories of provenance, the handmade signs and the seemingly added dirt. It's the lavender oil factory store in Provence, the oddly expensive wine store at the vineyard. Buying is the tailored suit made from Suit Supply where the consultation is part of the experience.

What to do about it

Move to one extreme to thrive. Retailers need to establish which type they want to be and work hard to maximize that. Either systematically reduce complexity at every turn, or add it in the most delightful way. Don't get caught in the middle.

Young older people

Businesses are obsessed with Millennials. We talk endlessly about how to target them, how to make them feel at home in the working world, about how they behave, how they are different. Yet I think we're after the wrong people. The over-50s have 80 per cent of the developed world's wealth and yet we make zero effort to talk to them.

Millennials are not the creators and makers of all trends; life doesn't start with them and move out.

We have another idea in marketing, that teenage years are formative, that we grow up to be loyal in later life to brands we experienced when we were young. The few brands I now care about (Rag and Bone, Virgin Atlantic, Design within Reach, Waitrose, Standard Hotels, Sonos, Tesla) have just come to me in the last year or so. This has always been the case. Brands change, products change, people change. This is not a cycle that is slowing. Quite the opposite.

I'm not sure if anyone in marketing has noticed, but old people don't look or act like they once did. We're moving from Victor Meldrew to Helen Mirren, a generation of incredibly energetic, fantastically confident, wise people who just happen to have pretty much all the money in the world and plenty of time to spend it.

References

Loras, S (2015) Why have QR codes taken off in China?, 15 November, available from: https://www.clickz.com/why-have-qr-codes-taken-off-in-china/23662/ [last accessed 11 December 2017]

Marketing Charts (2016) Digital devices now influence the majority of US in-store sales, 20 September, available from: https://www.marketingcharts.com/industries/automotive-industries-70812 [last accessed 11 December 2017]

The Economist (2016) Bots the next frontier, 9 April, available from: https://www.economist.com/news/business-and-finance/21696477-market-apps-maturing-now-one-text-based-services-or-chatbots-looks-poised [last accessed 11 December 2017]

09
Preparing for the new world

In a book that's full of bold statements and personal opinions, no chapter fills me more with dread, a sense that I'll look idiotic in the future, than a chapter based entirely around predicting the future. The internet is ablaze with smart people making silly predictions, so why would I run the risk of making a fool of myself?

The answer is twofold. Firstly, I think it's vital that companies start looking ahead more. We will spend all our life in the future, so it's worth taking time to think about it and try to establish what we can and can't predict and what confidence levels we have. And secondly, I'm concerned about the degree to which technology-led and data-driven people and culture seem to 'own' the idea of predictions. I see far too much written, so many clear projections, based on what appears to be remarkably little familiarity with the human race. So this chapter is here to help shine a guiding light into the future, help stimulate debate, show what we know but also what we've no idea about. This chapter is about helping people understand the future state that businesses, brands and people could face. I encourage you to use this to establish threats and opportunities and to leverage this to make proper changes now.

Looking further forward is more important than ever

If we look back from these accelerated times, we draw comfort from the knowledge that things have never changed so fast before. From new technology to changing consumer behaviour and media fragmentation, no wonder it feels difficult to keep up. Life has never been so fast.

The need to look ahead has never been greater. When you drive a car, or any vehicle, it seems sensible that the faster you are travelling, the further ahead you need to look. For decades, the prescribed answer has been agility. Companies adapted to change, with small nimble teams, comprising a mixture of specialists and generalists. But what if responding fast was now too slow? What if, in words widely attributed to former professional ice hockey player Wayne Gretzky, we skated where the puck is going?

If we are honest, how many roles in most companies have a forward focus? Typical jobs and processes are entirely based in the recent or distant past. Sales results capture the historical results of decisions made long ago; case studies showcase what agencies were capable of many years ago, from annual results to best practices; even forward planning exercises start with what's been done before. We copy what our competitors have made today, when the gears of motion started long ago. If we copy that now, we will be too late. If there was such a measure, the collective focal point of marketing and business people is firmly in the past.

And who can blame them? The fastest way for me to lose all credibility in a room is to come close to mentioning anything to do with seeing the future. The science of 'Futurology' seems as dubious as that of Scientology. The world of business needs more than ever to change its focus. We live in the age of insurgents, who use last-mover advantage to deploy the latest, best and cheapest technology and who take advantage of new behaviours.

We need collectively to get better at future planning, and improve the way we establish what are fads and what are shifts. We like to pounce on the short, simple, little things. We're quick to discuss Flappy Bird or Second Life, we instantly try to digest ChatRoulette, Meerkat, Periscope or Candy Crush, but often these things are not significant.

Instead, longer, more transformative, more human changes need to be understood. We need to understand what will last longer, have a greater material impact on business and commerce, customer service, economics and brands, and we need to plan accordingly.

So with that in mind, here are some ways to think more usefully about the future.

It's about empathy not technology

Trends may appear to be driven by technology, but more often than not they are about reflecting humanity. We may think selfies are both highly contemporary and rather odd, but they reflect the human need to build a social network, express who we are and create a peer and support group. We may think social media is new, but even the caves in Lascaux had a 'wall'. When you really understand people, you realize that it will be several generations before we'll be wearing technology on our faces, because, for human beings, eye contact and facial expressions are too important to be covered. Humanity and technology jar against each other. Even more subtle worn technology like smartwatches have limited appeal because for many people the wrist is vital real estate to tell the world who you are. Many like to use it to show their refined tastes, others like to show social status and wealth, yet smartwatches today seem to broadcast the wrong things. As things stand, they show the user is fascinated, or rather self-obsessed, by technology, or that they need to be kept up to date with everything; I'm not sure how attractive these signals are to many.

The best way to understand the future is to understand primal man and woman. We are driven to want to tell the world who we are, to form social bonds, to procreate, survive, and to have shelter, food and safety in order to do that. Brands and companies built on those tenets of life will do well.

You have to feel and smell your way into understanding the future. The past is a good predictor of the future, but the real skill is knowing what won't ever change and what is likely to. One of the hardest problems in life is navigating the territory between those who constantly cry that 'this time it's different' and those who frequently bark 'but we've seen this all before'. The way to deal with this is to just let your mind wander and let the dots join up.

Predictions are more about empathy and imagination than science. I'm lucky, as my role is based on travelling the world, listening and observing. You arrive in Paris to endless strikes from taxi drivers about Uber, you're in India hearing people talk about the exploding middle class, you see kids in Rio's favelas watching TV on a smartphone, or a self-service experience beyond what you ever expected in

Oslo, and you start to feel your way through the world and life and see how things should and could develop and unravel.

I'm amazed how many terrible predictions are made about the future. Amazingly, people who own Bitcoin predict it will do well. But these are not the people to ask; it's in their self-interest to create a future where they will prosper. I see a lot of predictions based on how people will behave in scenarios they can't even imagine. When you get a group of people to answer questions like 'would you ever buy a self-driving car?' or 'would you trust a robot to look after you?', you get entirely useless answers. Asking people for their opinions on things that don't yet exist is naive in the extreme.

We love interpreting data in a linear fashion and it doesn't work. The early uptake of the Amazon Echo can't be modelled around that of the smartphone and interpolated. Data does an excellent job of mapping the past and the current, but a terrible job for those who need to look ahead. 'Chartism' is rife in all elements of futurology and, by and large, it never works. Interpolation of data would suggest 3D TVs would be taking over the world, that Sodastreams would be found in every house, that the world should have more smartphones than people by now, that we would spend 24 hours a day watching TV.

Many trends exist as actions and reactions. It's the array of new technologies in our homes that make people in most countries demand more traditional housing that borders on pastiche. It's the time freed up by using Walmart or Amazon or Tesco that makes us want to go to the farmers' market (and it's interesting to note that farmers' markets are only ever in cities, never in the countryside). Because we ate lunch at our desk we want to cook tonight. Most trends have countertrends, and it's by understanding this that we unearth where many opportunities lie. If our shopping becomes boring, where can we get fun back into life? If we're staying the night in bland hotels, then how can businesses explore individuality?

Second-order and adjacent technologies

Innovation and progress never happen in a vacuum. It's far from a scientific experiment with one variable fixed. The future of electrically propelled cars isn't isolated against changes in software that allow self-driving cars to operate. Nor is it isolated against business models based on accessing rather than owning cars, or against a move towards businesses using improved telecommunications structures to allow more people to work from home, or the change in career expectations and personal goals that mean people may seek to freelance more.

The hardest thing about any prediction is seeing the unknown second- and third-order effects that nobody could have possibly calculated. As Carl Sagan said, and as supplemented by Kevin McCullagh's analysis of key technology changes, 'It was easy to predict mass car-ownership but hard to predict Wal-Mart' (McCullagh, 2017).

Who saw the rise of the mobile phone and then predicted emojis? Benedict Evans has a fascinating argument that electronically propelled vehicles could save thousands of lives by reducing cancer deaths, because of the resulting vast reduction in gas station infrastructures that encourage the impulse buying of cigarettes (Evans, 2017).

We need to think of what will happen to flying when and if VR headsets take off. What will happen to mobile commerce in a world of 3D printing? What will happen to electronic scooters if we use multimodal transport apps? Unanticipated consequences are everywhere. If robots start taking over many human jobs, will they create more jobs in new fields, will we earn money from the taxes they pay on the income they generate for free? What happens to the meaning of life in this situation? Do we find more time to watch cat videos or finally get around to writing poetry and reading Russian literature?

The key to all predictions is to establish what all these dots do when aligned. It is balancing feeling with data, imagination with technology knowledge, fixing what's certain and ideating around what is unknown. When you do that you can establish a cone of plausibility and that is where some of these longer-range views that follow have come from.

Anticipatory computing and seamlessness

Broadly speaking we've had three eras of the web so far, each defined by three distinct behaviours and each with their own winners and losers. It's the next era where things get interesting.

The portal era

The first era of the consumer internet was the era of portals: the internet as a web-based magazine.

This era was dominated by the same players that ruled the pre-digital world. We simply took the information that had once been printed on paper and placed it on a screen. In this pre-2004 world, players like Yahoo, Netvibes, Excite, Lycos or AOL became our gateway to the internet, saving it as documents and arranging information in directories much like filing cabinets. We'd taken pre-digital-world structures and replicated them. Our behaviour in this era was similar to reading magazines or newspapers; we had a relationship with a provider, and largely went down the rabbit hole that was their content. This was an internet based on homepages, bookmarks and a daily routine: the internet mainly as words, simple images and infrequent linking out.

The search era

The second era was one of search when the search bar became the new gateway to the internet. From 2004 onwards, the first destination we would often visit wouldn't be a page full of information, but a search bar and nothing else. For the first time we were now in control. PageRank from Google became the enabler, but we were still the navigator. Information wasn't pulled through to us, we had to go find it, but everyone could contribute and the popularity and depth of the internet exploded.

This was the era of the deeper, richer, more democratic web. Content was hidden in messy structures, but was pulled up to our browsing layer by complex search algorithms. The internet in this era became about surfing. We skimmed the top of the internet, opening 10 then 20 then 30 browser windows at a time. The winner of this era was Google, the shop window for all browsing, the owner of most data, the customer interface to later own advertising.

The social era

The big winners in the third age were social networks. From Facebook to LinkedIn, Twitter to Snapchat, the dominant new form of browsing is based on what people we know have shared, suggested, broad-casted, retweeted or liked. From 2006 onwards, it's these companies that have done best at recruiting users and traffic.

We do of course still search, but usage levels over the last few years are down. We increasingly use the internet on mobile phones, but much of our time on the mobile web is spent on social media. While we may dip into the micro-portal of a banking app to find our balance, we're probably spending more time on Facebook, WeChat or other socially oriented and curated experiences.

The social age so far has been the most complete and mature version of the web. We've killed homepages and instead, when we go onto the internet, because of friends or people we follow or smart algorithms, we are presented with a version of information and the internet that is likely to be most relevant to us. Our search results are based on history, our Facebook feed is scarily based on what we would most like to see, or at least find most palatable, our Twitter feed is a less sophisticated and more pure pull-through version of what people we have chosen to listen to think we should see.

The Internet of Things

The main driver of the next stage of the internet comes primarily from data, but also from better processing of it and smarter actions. If the internet has always been about connections between people and information, the next paradigm is one of things being added to the mix.

We could soon be in an era where computers effectively become a support function for us. They become an ambient assistive layer.

A well-known expression from software developer Eric Raymond, and reported by Benedict Evans, states that, 'A computer should never ask the user for any information that it can auto-detect, copy or deduce' (Evans, 2016).

As more data is recorded and shared by more things, increasingly we need to tell the computer less.

The big hope of computing in the near future is that a vast increase in sensors, a vast improvement in how they talk to each other, a far more robust system for looking at past behaviour and making predictions, and (most importantly) a more progressive attitude from people towards what we can rely on computers to do for us, will all mean that computing becomes personalized, assistive and predictive.

This offers incredible opportunities for brands to advertise better, and for companies to change their business models by offering to serve these new expectations. As time goes on, we have less time and more choices to make. While technologies like voice interfaces are going to reduce the cognitive burden required to make things happen, what will be even more transformative will be automation of decision, and the notion of 'light nudges', or key contextual suggestions. It's fascinating for businesses to think how they can leverage the opportunities that this smartness will create. How can you get people to order more products? How can you get people to invest in more expensive systems? How can you make everything as slick, and seamless, as possible?

The predictive web: the Th'Internet

We see small signs of this today. For example, Google scans your e-mail and can automatically track flights and add them to your calendar. At some point everything should connect and just work, but before then, we're stuck between the dumb and the smart – the interim of things, which I call Th'Internet.

Soon we will see the world get smart around us. At the moment we have Amazon's personal assistant, Alexa, and Philips personal wireless lighting, Hue, which means I have to think a little bit more about lighting my home than when I simply used a light switch. But soon perhaps when I return home on a Monday night in January my favourite jazz music will be playing and the lights will be on, but dimmed, and I'll enter a preheated home that could tell when I'd be back. This raises fascinating user interface challenges. Does it do it automatically? Does it nudge me and ask 'Monday night setting?' and I have to say yes?

Anticipatory computing will make constant micro-predictions about what we are likely to do, need, and want. Many aspects of our lives will become seamlessly assisted by thin contextual information and smart suggested options or nudges. This offers incredible opportunities for brands to advertise better and for companies to change their business model and offering to serve new expectations.

Privacy trading

'Privacy may actually be an anomaly' said Vinton Cerf, co-creator of the military's early internet prototype and Google executive (Ferenstein, 2013).

For so long we've done all we can to guard privacy and our personal data. Increasingly we may first give up the battle and then focus on trading it for something of value.

Living at a time when reality TV stars continue to get rich, when it seems every Instagram user wants to get paid to be an influencer, it seems rather strange to both want to be known, to be popular and envied and also to not have anyone know anything about you. Privacy is a complex matter, but is it realistic to share so much for so long and then be shocked when little about your life is a secret anymore?

We are on the edge of a divide: some of us guard privacy furiously, some of us begrudgingly let go of it, and some of us have no understanding of it nor a real need to defend it. I've got a feeling that soon the battle to maintain privacy will become difficult, that the benefits of sharing data will become so clear that most people will embrace the idea that privacy is an asset to trade.

The mistakes we made when we were young are being swept aside by the torrent of time: the errors of children today may manifest themselves on servers around the planet, as opposed to within the small confines of our schools or communities. But how can kids miss something like privacy, a concept they've probably never known?

We have traded privacy for longer than we realize. We have had store cards that record what we have bought, that have aggregated and sold the data anonymously, and then used this to target us with special offers while giving us money off. When we use our phones and Google Traffic, we share our speed and locations and benefit from the greater good. Browsing and search histories are used to give us more relevant data; healthcare is based on using patient data and history; companies like 23andMe use DNA records. Through all these we have gently eroded our privacy and got little in return.

I think in the near future we may swing to embrace privacy trading more emphatically. There are three key elements to consider.

Trust

Seemingly weekly data breaches and hacks mean we are going to need companies with robust records for data safety and governance. It's most likely that we will think of companies such as Amazon or Google, and far less likely Facebook, to record, store and manage our data for us. If we trust these companies with our most personal details, then we have a potential foundation for this concept.

Transparency and control

For this to work, companies will need to be clear, honest and transparent about what data they are keeping, what they are using it for, and to continuously offer the chance for us to control and modify it. Knowing you've bought a TV is one thing; knowing your blood test results or genetic code is absolutely another. If health insurers, for example, could ever access some of this information, we'd have absolute mayhem.

Value

So if the key is making it worth people's while, what can be offered in exchange for the great value of the data recorded, stored and used?

While we talk a lot about data today, the world doesn't reflect an environment where companies know too much. I'm shown ads for watches I bought a while ago, others for rental apartment complexes I now live in; you buy a tape measure and Amazon thinks you want to avidly start collecting them.

I enjoy the mental experiment of assuming that companies know pretty much everything about me. I'm 38 and travel a lot. Would this be a terrible world? What if someone could find a way to show me, rather than mesothelioma class-action suits or TV ads for Viagra or Chevrolet leasing, ads for a new Burberry man bag, or a new app that offers a better doctor's experience or a stunning ad for a new lifestyle clothing company that makes edgy simple fashion? I know these companies are prepared to spend a fortune reaching me. The advertising inventory would be worth even more if I was shown fewer ads. If I was shown slightly fewer but more relevant ads, I'd be far happier, the brands would be far happier, and the TV channels who sell advertising space could make far more money at the same time.

Let's assume my bank and credit card company know where I am at all times, and perhaps my airline, the hotels I use, or the retailers I visit also know. In fact, why can't everyone know where I am?

On a conceptual level I don't have an issue with us exploring how this data can be used. I'd love to see people focus on how this data could be stored and managed in a way that works for everyone. Maybe I don't mind my credit card spend being shared with advertisers, my TV habits shared with banks. Maybe I just want things to work around me and this helps.

As part of this system we will soon find friction removed from life in return. It's amazing today that passcodes and user IDs and other accounts are still typed in every single day and often several times a day. It's estimated $16 billion is wasted in time each year just with lost passwords (Loftus, 2010). In the future things will be seamless, with passwords fading into the background, and our face, fingers, voice, heartbeat, or other mechanisms used to gain entry seamlessly.

The main idea here is that we stop the assumptions from the past. We have always trodden carefully around privacy as if it's a beast that we may wake up. We have figured out subtle ways of doing little things in the background that offer no clear value, but won't be noticed. We can start the conversation in a different way. We can work around what we can maximize as value to give to people. We can have much more honest and open conversations with people about what information they may be willing to share with us, and, assuming that they have our trust, we can create more personalized and better experiences for them.

The benefits of privacy trading for companies in the future are clear: as we get more data from more people, we can help them make decisions like never before. We can offer better experiences: hotels that can welcome you as you check in, without any information required from you, and planes that can be kept waiting for you because they know your frequent flyer status.

Smartness in the cloud

Devices are becoming more intelligent and more helpful, and the cloud has enabled a smartness to pervade the technologies we use every day.

There is much debate about the future of smartness. It's probably the Amazon Echo that first showed the idea in practice. Amazon Echo is one of the smartest and cheapest devices currently available. It is actually just a speaker and an internet connection. The speaker here, like the Google Home or Apple HomePod, merely becomes a relatively dumb access point to the smartness in the cloud. We see this everywhere. Tablets these days are relatively cheap and don't become obsolete so fast, PCs are stubbornly cheap and oddly slow to improve, software like Adobe now runs in the cloud and not on the device. Our data increasingly is elsewhere, on Google Docs or Dropbox.

Moving smartness into the cloud facilitates a new system and way of thinking. The smartness is removed from devices and is now found in the systems and structures behind them. A good example is contactless payment with bank cards on the London Underground. In this system you are not buying a ticket digitally, you never own a ticket, you merely get permission to enter and permission to leave, and when you leave you are billed for the travel directly to your bank account. Imagine if, rather than passports, we carried nothing: all records were stored in the cloud – permissions, visas, entry stamps – and instead of us carrying a document, we were just identified by fingerprints like the clear entry system in the USA allows. What if we just used our face, like Face ID, to board planes and never carried tickets? What if we never needed to use a phone or metro card to get on a bus or leave a system and we were just automatically billed by our phone company for the distance we travelled, the method and the time of day based on how far we went, established by GPS routers or even sonic technology like Chirp?

We need to get better at thinking about digital transformation in a more effective way. Credit cards are not photographs of money that people exchange; they are entirely new systems and structures built on top. Let's rethink all systems this way. Perhaps the cash of the future is not a digital wallet but your face or a unique identity band. Perhaps we don't carry the tech any more. It will be interesting to see what happens around the world as companies build for this.

Increasingly life isn't about coincidence; it's about algorithms. News is now automatically selected based on what we like, will click on and most likely share.

Advertising is slowly not only placed and bought with algorithms and programmatic technology but also created automatically and specifically for you. We all know retargeting, and the slippers that stalk you around the web, but increasingly there is technology like Dynamic Creative which can render out a personalized display of video ads based on your search history, weather, stock market performance, locations, and even things like stock levels in local stores. You may be shown ads for convertible cars on sunny spring days, or a pricier watch when the Dow hits new heights. Ads can be rendered out from billions of permutations to show you directions to the local store and even offer personalized pricing based on what the software thinks will make you take action.

Demographic shifts

One of the most profound, impactful and interesting trends that I'm not covering in detail in this book is the huge change that technology is having on society.

I'm not best placed to do this. I'm not an expert in this field, but I want to ask some questions which many need to ponder as we look ahead. These changes are not widely discussed because I sense that most people are in denial.

People worry about the significant changes in the distribution of population. Whether it's the demographic time bomb of having people give up work at the same age, then living longer in retirement while requiring more expensive healthcare to keep them alive, or the changing nature of the middle class and the increasing income gaps between the rich and the poor – these are not topics that many people enjoy listening to at conferences.

A tech-driven future is becoming divided

We face a world that seems more divided than ever. I don't think its root and only cause is technology, but technology is certainly catalysing and exaggerating social change and creating worrying futures for many in jobs and countries that face change at a pace faster than can be dealt with. It seems we are on the threshold of great change.

It's fair to say that at most times in human history, technology has been seen as a force for good, and as a way to progress to a better state. Technology has improved health, given us luxury in many forms, be it time or through the medium of more stuff to own. For years the world of business was a world led by business people. They had vision but they were never 'geeks'. It's been a world of Jack Welches, Henry Fords, Andrew Carnegies, Richard Bransons, even Steve Jobs was more entrepreneur than hacker. For a considerable length of time, scientists and 'geeks' didn't shape corporate strategy: they made it happen.

Now, for the first time in history, the geeks are calling the shots, shaping the future, and they understand technology perfectly. But they are not like the entrepreneurs of the past. These are not people who seem to have an innate understanding of people – far from it. If anything, the more objective mathematical precision required to be successful in technology and coding almost requires that these people don't understand the subjectivity, emotion, and nuance of the human character. It creates for me a very worrying combination of circumstances. It seems that for many people the future of humanity lies not in connecting communities and building bridges between different people, but rather trying to escape, bury under, or fly over the issues that these new problems have created.

Extremism

We have long lived in a world where different people held different views. We have long had newspapers that represented different political sides. But we tended to know that. If you were a Fox viewer, you knew that you were seeing the right-wing side of the debate. A CNN viewer would know that they were seeing the left-wing side of the debate. But you would know that two sides existed. The same is true with newspapers – you would go to the newsagent, and see a variety of headlines, each designed with a particular audience in mind.

The terrifying aspect of the modern media platform is that we do not get exposure to how different people receive the same news, in different ways. A glance over someone else's Facebook feed may enlighten you to an entirely different series of events, or different feelings, about the same events. It means that people can have quite strange views, and think that they are rather normal. The abundance of material written in the world, the incredible incentives that exist for people who write extraordinary articles, mean that you can pretty much have any opinion in the world, and feel like it is somehow normal – whether it is thinking that vaccines cause autism in children, that the earth is flat, that climate change isn't happening, or that 9/11 was a government conspiracy. You can have any opinion, and be lulled into a false sense of normality.

While this doesn't have any direct impact for business leaders, or lead to any opportunities, it helps us understand the context in the future, when we are likely to see greater divides between different types of populations. Perhaps we will see brands seek to define their audiences by particular belief systems and political opinions, but the main learning here is that we are not about to become more connected. Every year, we have more countries in the world. Every year, new regions threaten to separate – we see Brexit, Catalonia in Spain tried to break away – the world is not becoming more connected.

Death of the middle class

Many people now think the middle class is a historical anomaly, that its rise was surprisingly recent, happening in the mid-19th century, and that it is fast crumbling. It's normal to assume the world we see today is how life has always been, but for most of human history this middle-class layer has not existed.

Yet many people think a large, growing, confident middle class is vital for growth. Henry Ford first realized that if his skilled hard-working labour force were unable to afford the product they were making, then it limited the chance of success. Peter Drucker thinks the entire point of an economy is to create a middle class (Drucker, 1993).

While many in the USA love the idea of 'trickle down' economics, there is a growing 'middle out' movement: a group of people who think that the wealth from the rich flowing down just doesn't work. The evidence of trickle down at the moment for many is scant. Then the McKinsey Global Institute produced a report, *Poorer than their Parents: Flat or falling incomes in advanced economies,* which shows a growing trend in stagnating or declining incomes for middle-class workers. And it shows it's global (McKinsey, 2016). The report revealed that in 25 advanced economies around the world 75 per cent of people suffered from income reduction in the last 9 years. In the 12 years before only 2 per cent of homes saw income come down. The maths showed that, between 2005 and 2014, 540–580 million people have earned less.

Artificial intelligence

Artificial intelligence (AI) is one of those terms that has a habit of being used indiscriminately and abundantly, a sort of press release filler to imply something is better than it used to be, more advanced, worth paying extra for.

One of my favourite quotes is Justice Steward Potter talking about adult material in the now famous case of *Jacobellis* v. *Ohio* in 1964. In it, when talking about the nature of pornographic material, he accepted that he didn't really know what it was, but in his words, 'I Know It When I See It'. Artificial intelligence it seems today is almost the opposite: you can have a great theoretical understanding of what it is, but absolutely no idea when you experience or see it.

One of the reasons that our landscape has seen the term AI prolif-erate is because it's deeply exciting and has profound implications for many aspects of life. The other is because it's actually a term so vague that it diminishes its meaning and understanding. *Encyclopædia Britannica* calls it: 'Artificial intelligence (AI), the ability of a digital computer or computer-controlled robot to perform tasks commonly associated with intelligent beings' *(Encyclopædia Britannica*, 2017).

You can see now why AI is so commonly used to describe something that seems to be very advanced or uses algorithms in a profound way, or makes decisions for us, or involves automation. If your job is based on Excel, you are most easily replaceable (number crunching); if it's about moving things around (manual labour) you are safer; MS Word (communications), you will last even longer; but it's PowerPoint-based jobs (ideas and creativity) that will be safest of all.

Yet really, AI is best thought of less as a technology, but more as a disparate array of technologies underpinned by a few common elements. More data, faster processing, the ability for computers to learn or get better, and some degree of advanced logic or reasoning. In my view it's more usefully thought of as a philosophical approach towards computing and problems.

It's easier to think of AI less as some buzzword and more as a way of thinking about business transformation, in the same way that electricity has changed business. In fact, what we have learned from how to apply electricity and how to apply digital thinking and processes can be applied perfectly to the concept of AI. If we add AI into some roles and departments, if we apply it to what we have already, we once again will have missed its transformational power.

What AI really needs to do is recreate the entire canvas of opportunity. Companies using AI first need to consider what the role of that company will be in an AI-driven world. What value do they need to add? In this new world, what ideas, what decisions and what stuff do they need to make, and what will be the roles of humanity and of machines? If AI doesn't lead to changes in company structure, if it doesn't elevate the role of automation in a big way, if it doesn't lead to significant job changes, then it's been done wrong. AI is more like root canal than a polish. It will be painful, but it's what is needed.

It was Ginni Rometty, CEO of IBM, who said that AI should really stand for Augmented (human) Intelligence (Pearson, 2017). The time seems to be upon us, right now, to question how far AI should transcend historical human endeavours such as law, ethics, and an effective contribution to society. If we get it wrong, then we end up either overplaying or underplaying the role of AI, with damaging ramifications either way. Our view of AI will, of course, change along with society, but what I ask from this book is that we think about where all of this leads us.

Further, although I have split out the preceding sections as discrete topics, I would like the reader to consider how they can be intellectually conjoined. For example, one way to combat extremism is for the big content platforms – Twitter and Facebook – to use AI in such a way that they flag up articles and people of note that lie *outside* of an extremist user's filter bubble. This is a perfect example of AI being a way to augment human intelligence and to both broaden and challenge our horizons.

References

Drucker, P (1993) *Post-Capitalist Society*, HarperBusiness, New York

Encyclopædia Britannica (2017) Artificial Intelligence [online] 12 January, available from: https://www.britannica.com/technology/artificial-intelligence [last accessed 6 December 2017]

Evans, B (2016) AI, Apple and Google [online] available from: https://www.ben-evans.com/benedictevans/2016/6/23/ai-apple-and-google

Evans, B (2017) Cars and second order consequences [blog] Ben Evans, 29 March, available from: https://www.ben-evans.com/benedictevans/2017/3/20/cars-and-second-order-consequences [last accessed 6 December 2017]

Ferenstein, G (2013) Google's Cerf says 'Privacy may be an anomaly'. Historically, he's right, TechCrunch, 20 November, available from: https://techcrunch.com/2013/11/20/googles-cerf-says-privacy-may-be-an-anomaly-historically-hes-right/ [last accessed 6 December 2017]

Loftus, J (2010) Are passwords a waste of time?, *Gizmodo*, 04 November, available from: https://gizmodo.com/5514469/are-passwords-a-waste-of-time [last accessed 6 December 2017]

McCullagh, K (2017) Cities are about to change forever. Here are 3 key decisions they must make, *Fast CoDesign* [online] 05 May, available from: https://www.fastcodesign.com/90123848/cities-are-about-to-change-forever-here-are-3-key-decisions-they-must-make [last accessed 6 December 2017]

McKinsey (2016) Poorer than their parents? A new perspective on income inequality [online] July, available from: https://www.mckinsey.com/global-themes/employment-and-growth/poorer-than-their-parents-a-new-perspective-on-income-inequality [last accessed 6 December 2017]

Pearson, N (2017) The business case for augmented intelligence [blog], *Medium*, 26 January, available from: https://medium.com/cognitivebusiness/the-business-case-for-augmented-intelligence-36afa64cd675 [last accessed 6 December 2017]

10
Tooling ourselves for the future

It is not the most intellectual of the species that survives; it is not the strongest that survives; but the species that survives is the one that is able best to adapt and adjust to the changing environment in which it finds itself.
MEGGINSON, 1963

The truth is that the more you know about AI, the less certain you can be as to its future or meaning. How the technology will develop is unknown, and how it will combine with others to create second-order effects is even less clear. We can easily dream of the singularity, where the pace of change gets so fast, computers create computers and 'take over', yet the robots we see today are less capable than two-year-old humans. We worry about computers becoming self-aware, but my printer typically isn't aware of my laptop.

Chapter 9 was meant to provide inspiration, designed to trigger feelings, and depict as clear a demonstration of the possible future. It's a great way to evaluate potential business models, to trigger thoughts to plan and stress-test scenarios. It's food for thought, it's nourishing and perhaps a touch inspirational.

Yet we need to understand what we don't know. We need to tool ourselves for uncertainty.

This chapter is the end of the theme on the future. It's here to explain how we can best be broadly suited to change; it considers some ways of thinking about change and ways to maximize the chance of success in unpredictable scenarios.

Unprecedented levels of unpredictability

It's amazing to me to think of the life before the consumer internet. Forget its military roots that go back earlier. Let's think of a moment in time around the mid-1990s and imagine in retrospect what we'd expect the internet would do. Let's say someone spoke about a system that connected the whole planet, something nearly free to access, something that a device for $10 could draw upon, anywhere. Let's imagine we spoke of a system everyone could upload to, near instantly. A system that would include images and videos and all human knowledge. That you could use to speak or write to anyone, in real time.

The internet means the world is connected more tightly than ever before. We can now access anything ever made, known, written or recorded. An eight-year-old child in rural Africa with a $10 smartphone can access more than the richest person on Earth could in 2000. There is nothing we can't learn. We can now understand most languages on the planet near instantly, connect with people we could never have dreamed of before.

We should in theory be more educated, more skilled, and more empathetic than ever, and ignorance should become obsolete. One would expect us to feel more closely bound, more in tune with each other. It would be reasonable to think that bullying would be harder, that breaking the law would be less likely or that people who screwed over other people or partners would find a way for trust and reputation to be revealed more clearly. We'd expect more transparency, for corruption to be harder. We'd expect social change like we can't imagine. Women in rural areas could support each other more, bad businesses would go out of business faster. Lying would be harder than ever. You'd expect social mobility to increase as anyone anywhere with a dream and ambition could find the people, knowledge and resources to escape what would have been a prison of opportunity before.

Some of this has happened. We read about it in the news, but we read about it because it's newsworthy and unusual. In reality, we have become more segregated, more fearful, extreme views have been normalized. A device that one could only expect would bring us together now sees a world with nations breaking off into ever smaller groups. The UK wants to leave the EU, Catalonia wants to break apart from Spain, Trump's America seems less trustful and more divided than anyone could have imagined. While we have never had so many democracies in the world and fewer autocracies since the internet took off, we have also, with 195 separate nations, never had more countries.

We see a world becoming divided, hate fuelled, empathy starved, with fewer bridges being built and fewer examples of compromise. From Turkey to Germany, France to the UK, Sweden to Russia, the wealthy elite see their futures brighten, while an undercurrent of the masses become angry, seek to turn their back on globalization and immigration, and dream of the past. All the time many of the world's richest people are leaders in technology, but not empathy.

Never before has the power and potential for change been less understood. We see plummeting poverty around the world, the eradication of incredible diseases done ever more easily, we see the rising middle class in China, South America and Asia. Items that were once luxury are now cheap and accessible. The internet means the youth of sub-Saharan Africa can access a world-class education. Healthcare advice is dispensed freely. We have now never had more reasons to be optimistic and stronger reasons to be concerned for our welfare. What happens when the burgeoning middle class want cars, or to eat meat? What happens when global climate change submerges those in river deltas and tropical islands? What becomes of a society where children grow up texting friends and not meeting them? We have no idea.

Most changes in life are slow to notice, such as climate change. Futurists want to talk about VR headsets, cars as lounges, skyscrapers made from trees, they want to see what 3D printing or drones mean. It's the celebration of the physical manifestation of gadgetry. We'd be better off thinking about societal shifts, population movements, governance in the age of smartphone voting. We focus too much on technology, not on people; too much on software, not enough on ethics.

It seems the sad truth is that the future is more unpredictable than ever. We've never done a great job at predicting, and for most of the time interpolation has been easier than prediction. Our experience has been 'linear and local'. We are programmed to think linearly. Our pre-programmed way to consider the future, and to imagine what's next, has been one of incremental steps. We've developed an intuition based on the idea of a staircase. Having gone up five steps, we think we can predict the sixth and seventh, with each one expected to be roughly like the last.

Rethinking education

To foster a population best able to deal with a future we can't yet see, we're going to need to change education… a lot. The reality of the modern age is that I learned more in one year of a well-curated Twitter feed than in my entire master's degree. I have better relationships from LinkedIn than from university, and yet higher education is one of the largest industries in the entire world.

If we really think about it, if most people were asked what the role of education is, they would say something along the lines of it being there to best prepare kids for their future. It would be to give them the skills they need to get good jobs, to cope with life stresses, to be happy, prosperous, balanced, kind, empathetic people. It's fascinating to me that a seven-year-old in school today will be reaching key stages of their career at around the age of 35, which will be in the year 2040. It's clear to me that 2040 is an age we can't even come close to imagining. The amount of change between 1997 and 2018 has been so wild and unpredictable, and there are more signs that this change will accelerate than that it will slow down. The challenges that a person will face in this era are beyond our imagination. Yet this seven-year-old in school today is being put through an education process based not around the likely skills and traits they will need for a career in 2040, but one based around the needs of industrialists in 1840.

Businesses are now complaining about the poor skills of school-leavers and graduates (Berr, 2016). We've assumed the way forward is to ensure that more people study for longer, but I think that the changing world means that we need to prepare kids in a totally different way. It's the clichéd hope of the paranoid parent that teaching Chinese will best prepare kids for a future of different power structures in geopolitics, but is that essential in a world of Google Translate? Many think teaching kids to code is the solution, but won't software be written by software soon anyway? Our vision for the future needs to include more imagination. It's staggering to me how much the world has changed, and how little education has. The digital age means a different world.

Current schooling seems outward-in. We prioritize knowledge above all else. It is tested in exams. The best in school are those who can most easily recall information. Which was pretty helpful until now, when information is immediate, everywhere and abundant. In a world of fake news, being able to form opinions, criticize, evaluate, and see both sides of the story are far more vital than merely knowing things, absorbing stuff and parlaying it back robotically.

For kids growing up today, let alone tomorrow, we're living in a world where we outsource knowledge and skills to the internet. I'm not saying that it is a waste of time to have good handwriting when we're more likely to be interacting with voices and keyboards, but I'm not sure that it's a priority to be perfect at it.

Kids will struggle to communicate if they can't spell at all, but when spell-checkers auto-translate and software handles voice-to-text, maybe it's not something to take up much time. Maths and the logical thinking that we gain from understanding it is essential, but perhaps we need to think of it more philosophically and get to grips with reasoning more than memorizing processes.

These are not changes we have to make, but they are principles and assumptions that we should question. The future is less about what to remove, but rather what to refocus on. I believe that there are six key attributes to develop; both at school and also in the workplace these are values at the core of who we are. This is an inside-out approach to developing robust, happy, balanced people fit to embrace the modern age.

The core characteristics are typically developed while we are young and typically shaped by educational establishments, but it's vital that these values are imbued both in parenting as well as beyond school and for longer. These values and approaches not only will serve people well long into their careers, but should be nurtured, supported and recruited for in all companies.

The workplace will change more in the next 10 years than it has in the last 50, and roles that once relied on physical work will increasingly be automated. Roles demanding data input, routine calculation and Excel are likely to be replaced most quickly by algorithms. Customer service roles in many sectors may vanish, but roles in luxury customer service, requiring different skills and attitudes, may grow. We need to think imaginatively. Coding will soon be done by code itself, but creative problem solving may be more vital than ever. Increasingly, the world of employment focuses away from doing, and more towards thinking. The knowledge economy will need people armed with the following core skills to thrive.

Relationships

The reality of the modern working world will, for many, exist not as an employee, but as a creator of value through relationships. I don't need to know how to code or shoot in 360 degrees or buy rights to music, but I do need to know the very best people who can. Education for the future needs to focus on ways to ensure people can build lasting, trusted, human relationships. The current environment where text messaging replaces phone calls, where e-mails replace meetings, where a generation stare nonchalantly, lonely and in isolation into phones needs to be curtailed by a focus on relationships. We need to learn how to listen, how to converse again. Leaders and managers will succeed in the future by establishing a combination of two things. Firstly, it is key that they build strong, trusted relationships with a select number of key vital connections. A quick glance at LinkedIn shows an overwhelming abundance of people. People need to know how to filter out those who are less helpful and then how best to build deep, trusted relationships with the people that really matter. Secondly, at the same time people need to go wide. Progress happens from connecting dots in new ways, in linking subject matter expertise from disparate areas in new ways. A key skill will be in building broad networks across varied disciplines, and establishing a reputation to help this network grow. I personally don't enjoy the current climate of 'the personal brand', but having a personality and being consistent and charismatic with how you think and act, being known and trusted and top of mind are always going to help future-proof your career.

Keeping curiosity alive

Two of the best attributes about being young are, first that we don't know any better and will take risks and not fear judgement, and the second is a relentless and unwavering curiosity. We don't need to learn to be curious, we need to nurture it in our children, and, as adults, continually remind ourselves of its importance.

When smartphones access everything, what enhances our knowledge and depth of thought is curiosity. It fuels our interest and forms the need for relationships with experts. If there is one attribute that we are born with and yet dies as we mature, then it's our innate human thirst to know more. We must embrace this. The people who open Wikipedia to get tips on their holiday abroad and end up somehow looking at the world's longest rivers or runways, or the people for whom every browsing session ends up with 23 tabs open, are those who still feed this curiosity. Curiosity is exhausting and wonderful, and rarely discussed.

From schools to employers, teachers to parents, I'd love to see people get behind great questioning, wonderful listening and eccentric interests. We think we show the world how smart we are with the things we say, whereas most often it's great questions that reveal who we are. Too often in life people ask questions to take it in turns to speak; they use the time between them to think of what they will say next. We need to get better at loving to listen and doing so properly. We need to listen to what people are saying in order to understand, not, as is often the case in modern social media life, to reply.

More than anything else organizations on all sides need to really digest the power of curiosity. Curiosity is not eccentricity. It's not a side aspect to our personalities that seems fun and frivolous. It is the engine of progress, central to the accomplishment of everything we do. The first step is to ensure that organizations of all kinds understand its importance and systematically find ways to recruit it, promote it and benchmark for it. We need to celebrate people with odd interests. Put people's talents on display and be inspired. We need to promote self-learning, especially learning that does not involve certificates and documentation. I would love to see KPIs (key performance indicators) based on outside interests and side projects. It is vital that those who show curiosity in all forms are supported, whether financially or emotionally. More than anything else we need to have curiosity agendas, programmes to bring in outside speakers, group trips to strange museums, team away-days in fascinating locations and with wonderful stimuli.

As we learned earlier, disruption happens when different ways of thinking come together, when people question things based on a new viewpoint. In the future, it is companies and leaders who have a breadth of passion, knowledge and skillsets, and the adaptability that results from it who will be most successful.

Fostering agility

We can't begin to imagine a career in 2020, let alone 2030. We've no idea what skills will be needed, what jobs will exist. It's a bold person who thinks that life will be slower. We're all going to have to get better at being more malleable and adept at change. It's not beyond the realms of imagination that even a 25-year-old today may have 30 different jobs in several different careers in their life. They may earn money from 10 companies at the same time. We need to get better at this flexibility.

In today's world we tend to find that algorithms and society shield us from the unknown. We unknowingly seek out people we most easily get on with, we read the news we find most comfortable and hang out in bars where people like us go. We don't think we are doing it but we do. At this time social networks reinforce this. We read opinion pieces that are the most palatable, most agreeable, our news diet becomes fast food, quickest to hit the pleasure receptors and most easily digested. We need to get better at working mental muscles, moving our bodies and minds to new positions.

Equally, in work, we talk about 'fluid' structures, of 'scrums' and agile teams and it all makes sense. But what if it wasn't about this?

Decisiveness

In addition to being more comfortable with the new, I think we need to get much better at making decisions.

We need the courage to make more decisions, more quickly and with more commitment. I see companies paralysed by the fear of bad choices, living endlessly in indecision. I see companies needing to make informed decisions swamped by data. I see the result of decisions leading to inaction. We live at a time when making terrible decisions, based on bad data and bad understanding of data, isn't punished because it was data-supported. We think data will light the way but increasingly it's blinding us.

At the same time, the reward for moments of genius, based on superb ideas, founded in a spark of creativity and deep empathy are zero because many think of it as fortunate at best, and reckless at worst.

All of the time we undermine the quality of feelings. If you ask a world-class cricketer to explain how they know when to swing, they look confused. They can't explain why, they can just feel it. Yet on further analysis they are analysing subconsciously far more data than they know. The bounce of the pitch, the humidity, the bowler's body language, the shape of the wrist. We can easily dismiss what is innate because it's unknown and unexplained.

More than any other attribute, indecisiveness is rooted in culture. Companies often have a culture of insecurity, of blame, of the need to appear safe in the role by not being noticed. I would love to see organizations embrace those who seek not to reduce risk, but to maximize the progress they make. A culture where people at all levels are empowered to make appropriate decisions will be faster. Companies should celebrate people who take risks, we should reward those who learn fastest, indecision should be a bigger crime than well-intentioned decisions that turn out badly.

In this environment meetings will be used less as places to share information or social bonding and more as key points in a process to get people to discuss and then decide en masse. Jeff Bezos is a master at creating a workplace based on smart choices. People get to speak, listen, disagree but commit. He talks of the need to understand differences between decisions you can easily go back on and those you must stick to. Jeff talks about the need to make decisions with the right amount of information: 90 per cent of the information needed means you are likely to be running too slow, less than 70 per cent means you don't know enough to be informed (Bezos, 2017).

With all this we need a vision of what we are trying to accomplish, but we need to be flexible. We need to be certain at all times of our mission in our role, but always uncertain of the route there. But that journey always starts with walking, even if not always in the straightest line.

Building empathy

We need to know what it's like to be different, how to relate to each other, and how to exceed the expectations, hopes and ambitions of others. In a world more divided and polarized than ever, we need to build bridges and commonalities. Empathy is our tool to do so.

Empathy is hard. It's relatively difficult to put yourself in someone's position, but this isn't true empathy. True empathy is not about moving yourself into their position: it's imagining that you are *them* in *their* position, in the sense that you are taking into account *their* values and life experience, and the whole of what makes them unique – not attempting to do that while still hanging on to what makes you and your experiences unique. Real empathy is understanding their very make-up, the things that make them who they are, the reason they do and choose what they do. It's extremely hard. We quickly ascribe stupidity to those people who choose very different things to us. We see people who are worried about immigrants and presume it's hate, when it may be they are worried about their own futures. We are quick to draw lines, to make generalizations, judgements, to be snobby. People who are different to us destroy the world that we want to see, one that we can understand most clearly and that makes sense to us.

In pragmatic terms we will see why parents in shopping malls don't want AR experiences on their phones; they want their kids to stop smacking each other in the face. We will see why the results of the satisfaction survey are skewed. We will notice that asking for an e-mail address to get content won't get real e-mails and why people won't read the great content we've made on mattresses or upload their haircut to a website.

Empathy is the strongest tool we have for predicting the success of marketing, businesses and ideas. It helps us form relationships, feel happy and be part of something. It's hard to develop, but vital to foster.

We really need to somehow foster tolerance and understanding, imagination and mental agility, such that we are better able to understand what others feel. It will help society but also help business. Firstly, I think business needs to elevate the importance of empathy. We focus so much on what is said and not what is understood, we tend to value extroverted behaviour not introverted, we like seeing the most material manifestations of what is done, not what was sensibly decided to not pursue.

We need to ensure that companies are diverse in their talent. Empathy comes from understanding the wonderful variety and depth of people, different cultures, races, classes, ages, and personality types. We tend to want to recruit and retain people who are easiest to get along with, who most readily like our ideas and think the same. This is a terrible way to make any worthwhile progress. In the search for the smoothest way to do business, we miss out on what is most useful for progress: friction. Disagreement is the energy that drives creativity; diverse thinking brings about improvements *because* it makes things hard, not in spite of doing so.

We need to get better at observation, take time to create processes and systems that allow people to get input properly. We have a passionate need to feel as if we are correct, so we view the world as it fits into our preconceived ideas, rather than the objective reality, which makes us feel odd, different and as if we don't understand it. We have to get better at the discomfort true empathy brings.

And my final thought is creativity, a subject I care about so deeply I want to bring it out separately.

The power of creativity

'It's much easier to be fired for being illogical than being unimaginative' (Sutherland, 2017).

Each and every one of us is born curious and creative. Schooling, friends, and 'proper jobs' somewhat dilute that, or (more realistically) it is metaphorically beaten out of us. We get told off for thinking too differently, for gazing out the window, for having the audacity to dream or being naive. Creativity when you're young is easy to maintain, but modern life tells you it's cheating, or not correct, or indefensible.

In the real world we get paid to solve problems or make or do things. It's never to remove steps or decide it's not right, or solve a problem a simpler way. The greatest lever of value that we've ever known is the power of an idea. Great design rarely costs much more, but it can unleash greater savings or increases in revenue than anything non-design based.

If Balfour Beatty is told a bridge needs to be built and asked to come up with an estimate of how expensive it will be, the answer isn't going to be a ferry or getting people to just drive around to another bridge and make the journey fun, or a far cheaper cable car or a way to charge people at peak times more to lessen the burden on the existing bridge.

We need to give paramount importance to creativity and ideas in the future, but my big worry is that we don't tend to think because thinking is cheap. It's unmeasurable and it's unknown and most people prefer certainty and spreadsheets and wasting money in a boring and defensible way. Most people do their jobs not to maximize the chance of something wonderful happening, but to minimize the chance of something bad happening.

I've a feeling that companies with vast resources rely on assets, processes and efficiency, rather than having to dig deep into the last resort, thinking or creativity. Which is odd because process and efficiency is a sure-fire way to get tiny incremental gains, where paradigm shifts in improvement come from innovation.

The comfort of properness and expense

Generally, very big problems are assigned very big budgets. After all, they are important. Big budgets allow every type of solution, from small fixes to huge constructions. Big budgets lead to an environment of fear – after all, something big is also serious. They lead to large teams, format processes, big decisions, pressure on shoulders. And it's precisely this culture and way of thinking in which creativity suffers.

Thinking is too cheap to be taken seriously, ideas seem flimsy in such an objective and formal atmosphere, creativity is too personal and any one of these outputs doesn't feel tangible enough to be taken seriously.

Can you imagine the courage you must have to suggest to a CEO or prime minister or president that the answer to your massive transport problem with a $10 billion budget is a $50,000 app? That the solution to education isn't billions on construction but a new aggregation engine? That the best way to deal with global warming and extreme weather could be to adapt to the effects, not trillions on stopping the problem? Can you imagine how vulnerable you'd feel?

Creativity needs constraints

The problem with money is that it creates too much comfort, too much process, too much conservatism, too much to lose. Have you ever noticed how successful some companies are despite limited funds?

Creativity comes from constraints, from people using ingenuity not power, thinking not construction, from people having to make something worth talking about, not paying people to spread the word. More than ever before it seems that the high cost of advertising in the modern era, as Robert Stephens, founder and chief inspector of The Geek Squad said, is the price you pay for an unremarkable product (Stephens, 2008).

I've never seen anyone fired for making a sub-standard product, spending a fortune trying to market it in a traditional way, and it not succeed. Yet I've seen many people fear for their jobs when saying something isn't good enough. I've been in countless corporate meetings where compliant people tell the boss what they want to hear, not what's most likely to lead to better outcome.

Having worked in advertising in the good old days – the long boozy lunches, the extravagant holiday parties, the nice shoots on beaches – the one thing I miss from those times isn't that laid-back attitude and money that swirled around, it's the confidence we had. We used to be there, paid to tell the client what to do. We were there as a trusted partner to save $100 million on launching a product that wasn't good enough. Our value was and should still be today in marketing to understand the consumer landscape and suggest creative ways to launch products.

A lack of money never stopped Nest from making the best thermostat on planet Earth. We see countless large companies make up for a lack of genius by using money to promote poor products and getting people to buy things that they don't really like or want and which is the most expensive thing on Earth.

Audacity

Imagination takes audacity. No market trends showed that a Smoothie for twice the price of a can of Coke and half the size would work. The makers of Red Bull made something tiny and highly priced and became billionaires. We can't use the past to predict the future. I sat in endless focus groups while testing Nokia smartphones and people hated them: they were too big, too pricey, had only two days battery life and, (I quote) 'Why would I want the internet on the move, I have it at home'?

Decision-making also takes audacity. Let's celebrate the unorthodox and the risky, let's nurture those who are lazy enough to find better ways, not those who work through problems. Let's celebrate risk, reward passion and those who persist while feeling vulnerable. Perhaps the wild ideas that didn't work still need measuring, but in a different way. We need to celebrate not just the weird, wild ideas, but nurture the weird, wild people who make them. And that, for many companies, is hard, because those people often don't belong in a box marked 'our values'.

The problem with contemporary decision-making is not just that we need to learn to say yes, but we also need to learn to say no. To say yes takes guts and an ability to dance with risk – to be aware of it, rather than to be scared of it. As I said in an earlier chapter, the safe space occupied by big companies allows risk to be outsourced, through the purchase and subsequent assimilation of start-ups. However, that risk needs to be brought straight into the C-Suite. If it doesn't happen, then you have – again, as I mentioned previously – leaders whose goals are centred on a safe route to retirement, rather than a risky but ultimately highly lucrative route to personal and corporate reinvention and success.

Encouraging risk also requires a change in how we think of reward. Leaders are often given both a golden hello and a golden parachute.

Many CEOs are given handsome pay-offs if they fail – and a 'mutual agreement to resign' from the board prevents them from being fired. They have no risk whatsoever. The opposite is true of founders, who often live off credit card allowances or remortgages to see their dream through, only finally realizing it on an exit or IPO (bearing in mind that most start-ups fail). For leaders in the C-Suite to really put their careers and intellect to the test, perhaps a little more personal sacrifice would sharpen the mind.

References

Berr, J (2016) Employers: New college grads aren't ready for workplace, CBS News, 17 May, available from: https://www.cbsnews.com/news/employers-new-college-grads-arent-ready-for-workplace/ [last accessed 6 December 2017]

Bezos, J (2017) Letter to Shareholders, available from: https://www.amazon.com/p/feature/z6o9g6sysxur57t

Megginson, L (1963) Lessons from Europe for American Business, *Southwestern Social Science Quarterly,* 44(1), 3–13, p4

Stephens, R (2008) Marketing is a tax you pay for being unremarkable, speech at the Customer Service is the New Marketing event, New York 4 February

Sutherland, R (2017) Mastering the future of marketing, speech at the dotmailer Summit, London 1 March

And in closing

11
A final focus on people

It's the end of the book so naturally I'm going to ask you to think about the desks you've seen lately. Seriously. What did the last hotel desk you checked in at look like? The last car rental counter? The last gate at an airline? What was the last till you paid at like? What does your desk look like at work? It's strange but we can see technology in the most enlightened fashion at the interface between people and key gateways.

Hotel check-in desks in slightly above average hotels are fascinating. Arriving at a hotel in the late 1800s you'd be dealt with by a person behind a large sturdy desk. It would have to be large; it was the barrier between you and all those heavy keys. The posher the hotel, the bigger and brassier the keys. The desk was there to store huge quantities of filing, records of visits, letters to patrons, and rules of the establishment. It was there to keep cash in a safe, to probably host some sort of till mechanism. My memory is poor.

By 1990 hotels were able to reduce the size of the check-in desk. Keys were smaller now, there was a large PC, a credit card carbon copy machine, a huge loud printer behind the desk. A few years later and, let's say, around 2008 the desks could be smaller still. They could or probably would have a laptop and credit card scanner and a key card programmer. But while the desks could have become smaller, they often hadn't. Desks were the visual language of the greeting: larger desks implied a grander and more sincere welcome.

Now, in 2018, funkier hotels have iPads, others have large Macs with glowing apples to broadcast slick and stylish design cues, but the desk remains big and bulky. We know that's the body language we are checking in with. Typically, you hand over a credit card for incidentals, and are asked to complete their paperwork for them. And that's fine because this is how life is.

I'm amazed how little rethinking we've done. We have replaced old technology with new, but changed nothing. We assume we need a desk, we assume someone needs to stand behind it, and that this is what arrival looks like. We assume it's okay to ask for things again that we have already asked for.

Car rental desks have followed the same evolution, cashier tills the same. We have embellished what we know is needed with new technology. The thing is: it's entirely wrong.

It's not about technology: it's about empathy

If, knowing enough about technology to know what's sensible, slick and reliable, we reconsidered the experience from a customer perspective, things would be wildly different.

What if we walked into a stunning lobby, and, rather than dragging our bags to a desk, we sat down and someone came to us with an iPad that we signed? What if they kept our credit card details from the booking we had made online earlier, rather than asking for them three times each visit? This is both a tiny and a hugely representative specific example.

What if car rental locations used iBeacons to know when you were arriving at their premises and then checked real-time car inventory and offered you special offers on upgrades with real-time pricing? What if you could upgrade by seeing the car you'd like at a sensible price and just swiping to the right? What if cashiers in stores came to you?

We persist in thinking about the technology first. When the brief becomes 'how can we use augmented reality headsets in airlines?', we get absurd examples like Air New Zealand demoing head-mounted solutions to help them understand the mood of passengers when really they would freak out any normal person. When the brief is 'how can we use chatbots?', we quickly establish a way to irritate our most valuable customers. We have to use technology to solve problems, find better ways to do things we've always had to do, but always in the service of the people who pay us money.

The best-in-class solutions are way more about empathy than they are about technology. They rely on challenging all assumptions of the past, on applying creative solutions around what people want.

Here are three ways to think about change and empowering your business to succeed.

Structure around people

It's weird to me that hairdressers don't work around office hours, or that car garages are reluctant to open on a Saturday, let alone a Sunday. Even in New York it's near impossible to see a doctor during the weekend or late at night. Clearly it suits the workers to work the same hours as the rest of the world, but these are industries designed to serve others. Posh restaurants won't let you take your bar tab to the dining room, because it's hard work for them to sort out. Retailers split into e-commerce divisions and physical stores because it's easier for them.

Since when has business been about the business more than it is about customers? Too often, if things are hard it is seen as an excuse not a challenge to be addressed. Every company needs to start working around customers not themselves. They need to create systems, policies and roles that seamlessly face the customer at all stages and retrospectively create structures around this to serve them best. We need to see new roles like 'chief experience officer' to support this.

A brand is what a brand does. It lives in the minds of people not on the brand onions of agency strategists. It's crazy that hotels spend $200 million easily and readily on advertising campaigns to tell the world they are friendly, and consider this a delightful investment to maximize, but spending the same on a training programme to ensure staff are happier and can serve people better is an avoidable cost to minimize. We regard reducing staff in a call centre as a sensible efficiency that will make customers cross in ways we can't measure, but spending money on advertising to bring them back is an investment whose success we can easily track.

This matters. People are more spoiled than ever, they demand more and will share more readily every experience they have, good or bad. A brand is now linked more to ratings online than to what ads tell people to think. Companies have long thought social media was a place to put messages, to tell people what to think about them, but today it doesn't work like that. If you think keeping customers happy is expensive, then consider the cost of unhappy customers. Your social media strategy in 2018 should be to ensure people have a wonderful experience, and this should permeate everything you do.

Focus on what matters

I've always thought the best innovation director would be an eight-year-old kid and their mean dad (it's always the dad's job to play bad cop). The eight-year-old would endlessly question, 'Why?', way beyond normal social acceptance, to really understand the problem. The dad would listen lovingly and then generally bark 'no'.

'Why' and 'no' are the most helpful words when we seek to drive change.

Innovation has always been misunderstood to mean more. We thought Nokia was innovative because they made 72 handsets a year, until Apple made a single one and it changed the world. The collective goal of companies has to shift away from doing extra, to work hard on doing less, better.

Let's help people make decisions. Let's help people buy. Let's remove steps. Automate what can be automated, make choice architecture simple. Innovation should be a reductive endeavour entirely focused on creating the best possible experience for consumers.

Generally speaking, people in roles doing new things like more. Saying yes means we get to show off more work we've done. Saying yes is good for everyone. It's much more profitable for an agency or consultancy to make a client an entirely futile Apple Watch app, charge them $100,000 to make it, help them invest $10 million on a campaign to promote it, than say no and save them a year of work and a fortune. We get world firsts by saying yes and even if it fails we can 'test and learn'.

I would love us to single-mindedly obsess about human beings, not on 'the next big thing'. Let's empathize with people in the shopping aisle, not cram a new feature into their lives. In a world that seems more complicated and faster changing than ever, let's focus on a few things, the things that matter. Let's do simple things well. No, simplicity isn't simple. Saying no to the right things is the real skill. But as an end goal it's essential.

Rethink the operating system

A common brief that comes my way is as follows: 'We've made an app, people are not using it and they say it's not very good. So how can we get more people to download it?' There is nothing more expensive that advertising and promoting a product that is not best-in-class. It clearly makes no sense, but it happens because of how many businesses operate.

Most businesses focus primarily on one thing: making things. It's how they have been structured, with roles like operations, finance, and procurement driving the majority of the processes and investments. With very few exceptions, marketing comes at the end of the process. The big budgets in R&D, the marvellous improvements in factory design, better procurement, new management thinking are all aimed at making better products, more cheaply and faster than before. By the time a product is made, all that those in the marketing department can control is how it is sold, not what is sold. In the whole process consumers are merely the people with the money who end up buying the items, after marketing and advertising has created customer interest in it.

The vast majority of companies still operate this way. 'Our factories have made curved screen TVs; go find a way to make people want them.' 'We found a way to make a lightbulb talk to a phone; make this seem sexy.' Very few brands or products are pulled by consumer demand, or co-created with proper research; they are all pushed out by departments and given to marketing to sell.

Products are made, market sizing is performed, likely price points are modelled and a potential yield is found. On this basis marketing budgets are decided, and then the chief marketing officer (CMO) is armed with ad agencies to invest this money in ensuring these targets are met. Creating demand was the business we were in.

It seems odd that we spend money pushing products uphill, not making products that sell themselves. In the words of John Willshire we should, 'Make things people want rather than making people want things' (Willshire, 2012).

Companies should find a new operating system that flips this on its head. Establish what people want, use this to inform marketing plans, design experiences and products based on this, decide marketing budgets required, use this to inform factories. Find ways to ensure customer service and experience are what matters. Kickstarter has shown how great products can find willing and enthusiastic audiences with ease. Companies around the world should focus less on pushing the next big thing and more on listening to consumers' needs, applying their knowledge of technology and design and making things for a group of eager consumers. My first ask: a washing machine that makes some sense.

A focus on empathy and design thinking

The well-funded enthusiasm of Silicon Valley is creating excitement and confidence in the idea that new companies know best de facto, and that if you understand coding and software you can take on anyone and win at anything. This goes unchallenged. Is software changing life in such a way that it's almost easier for a software platform or company with the world's best coders to become a better bank, than it is for a bank who has tried to recruit the best programmers? Can a car company become an expert in user experience and battery technology, faster than a design-led battery company can learn how to assemble cars? Can a platform like Netflix or Apple, Amazon or Facebook learn how to make great entertainment faster than TV companies or movie studios can learn how to create better distribution mechanisms? The race is on to see what is the best starting point, and often it appears that it's not being dominant in the past. I think what the incumbent industries need to leverage more is their experience in a particular category. In theory they know more than anyone else what people want and like.

Peak-end theory, usually attributed to Dr Daniel Kahneman, is where an experience or event is judged based only on two things: how we perform at the peak (the most intense point – good or bad) and at the end of the experience or event (Tran, 2015). Much like a chain is only as strong as its weakest link, so is customer service and our feelings about everything we have experienced.

I also proffer the thought that increasingly these days people are less forgiving than ever. Customers increasingly don't really care about how things happen or what the nature of the problem is. It's not okay to say that computers are running slow today or that there is an exceptional call volume or the computers should not have shown that the product was in stock.

In the age of computing and digital distractions, empathy seems to be a rare quality.

I once flew first class with Singapore Airlines. I was offered $300 bottles of champagne without a flinch, was given leather-lined amenity kits and expensive pyjamas for my $14,000 ticket. I guess that's what you'd expect. The departure lounge was a delight, perhaps a bit too much obsequious service, caviar on tap and more champagne, yet when I asked to borrow a phone charger, my boarding pass was confiscated until I handed it back. I'm not fussy, it clearly didn't ruin the experience, I got to Sydney alive, with all limbs, healthy and happy, but it's a rare glimpse into the world where empathy is lacking and yet money is rife. Why not buy phone chargers in bulk for a dollar, brand them with 'a gift from Singapore Airlines' and hope that I take it with me and bring back memories over the months I use it?

When you enter the amazing flagship Turkish Airlines lounge in Istanbul, with spectacular food and a dazzling interior design, you are met by a vast library of massive, wonderful books and a huge sign saying they are tagged for security and that thieves will be prosecuted. For all the technology in the world, for all the cost of journey mapping, of expensive hardware upgrades, customer service is often about the little things and it's about humanity and the softness of thoughts.

I think we tend to think that design is done by designers, that only when you have a black turtle-neck and a book about Dieter Rams can you dare offer suggestions. Maybe I'm weird but I think design is largely common sense, trying different things and thinking. I don't think it's that hard. From my frequent flying I've noticed that the ratio between arrival screens and departure screens in every airline lounge and every departure concourse is about 50:50. I can't think of any remotely normal use case where, after passing security, I care one iota about incoming planes, but there they are, freaking me out when I misread them.

In the wonderful and cathedral-like impressive new terminal at Barcelona Airport they have huge digital signs on most columns, not showing the time, but showing the temperature and the humidity. I can't think of any reason why anyone would want this.

We want to listen to customers, that's what improving service is all about. So I will never get over the arrogance of a 'hey, how was it?' e-mail, sent with the opening line 'we want to know how your stay was', from an @noreply e-mail inbox – and which simply wants me to click on a survey.

Final steps for success

Until the mid-19th century, artists in Europe kept their paint in pigs' bladders. It made carrying around paints extremely difficult. The bladders were very hard to close properly, and were likely to burst at any moment. It was because of these limitations and problems that artists were largely confined to painting in their own studios. It was the invention of the metal paint tube which changed virtually everything in art. Painters could much more easily paint outside. The impact of this simple technology was profound. Pierre-Auguste Renoir said 'without colours in tubes, there would be no Cézanne, no Monet, no Pissarro, and no Impressionism' (Hurt, 2013). It was the effect of natural lighting and the ability to paint anywhere which unleashed a special movement.

Technology changes societal norms. Until the common placement of elevators in 19th-century Paris, ground floors were grand and airy and the top floors were servants' quarters. Elevators literally turned apartment living upside down and a penthouse movement of grand conversions with grand views soon became a key part of Parisian society.

We are in the middle of the greatest change we've ever seen. Technology is empowering us to do near magical things on a daily or hourly basis. And quite frankly we appear to be lost in confusion. We are looking to each other for help, we are distracted by shiny things and we've collectively lost sight of what matters. To best deal with this, we can at best do something inconsequential and easy, and at worst we can hide. Can we please step up our game a little?

It's strange to me how few companies or industries feel especially excited about what new technology makes possible each day. As I have stated in earlier chapters, the cycles between 'ages' of technological change are getting shorter. It becomes harder to prepare for the longer term. Leading a company, a department, or even your own life thus becomes a principle of risk management.

I appreciate that I may appear contradictory when I say that we need to look at upcoming technologies in both a pragmatic but also a more daring way. Let me be absolutely clear on this point. Companies need to embrace the future of commerce, and the future of society. If they don't, then they will fail. If leaders cannot work with the new pace of change then I question their effectiveness in managing a business for the future. Change will come (it's already coming) and we all need to adapt – and quickly.

However, with that change comes a refreshed way in looking at how we view the customer. The end customer pays all our wages. Companies which fail at customer service will lose brand favourability, market share, shareholders, and market capitalization. That's not conjecture – it's a statement of fact. It means that we cannot look at touchpoints in isolation, even if technology defaults us to that behaviour.

In conclusion, what I have aimed at achieving in this book is a call to re-humanize not just technology, but our interactions with each other. With some irony, one might argue that this is the most important time in civilization to be human. Processes can be outsourced. Logic can be contracted out. Even intelligence can be engineered into printed circuit boards. But, the age-old tenets of reason, of creativity, of appreciation and of empathy will always be with us. It's now up to you, and me, and all of us to foster a more human world. We have incredible tools and more equipment at our disposal, which are more accessible, with more profound implications than ever before. We can either choose to embrace the power of the unknown, seek to create our own destiny, or we can pretend to, or we can hide. In a world where it is those best able to adapt who survive, who anticipate and embrace, and who confidently strive to accomplish what is only just about possible, I know what I'd do, and it's what I hope others will too. I'm confident it's this attitude that will be most successful in the age of Digital Darwinism.

References

Hurt, P (2013) Never underestimate the power of a paint tube, *Smithsonian Magazine,* May issue, available from: https://www. smithsonianmag.com/arts-culture/never-underestimate-the-power-of-a-paint-tube-36637764/ [last accessed 6 December 2017]

Willshire, JV (2012) Make things people want> Make people want things [blog] Smithery, 12 January, available from: http://smithery.com/making/make-things-people-want-make-people-want-things/ [last accessed 6 December 2017]

Tran, N (2015) Peak-end theory: How correct is our memory? [blog] Positive Psychology Program, 19 February, available from: https://positivepsychologyprogram.com/peak-end-theory/ [last accessed 6 December 2017]

INDEX

Note: Page numbers in *italics* indicate Figures.

CPSIA information can be obtained
at www.ICGtesting.com
Printed in the USA
BVHW061917140220
572401BV00014B/849